A Cryptography Primer

Cryptography has been employed in war and diplomacy from the time of Julius Caesar. In our Internet age, cryptography's most widespread application may be for commerce, from protecting the security of electronic transfers to guarding communication from industrial espionage.

This accessible introduction for undergraduates explains the cryptographic protocols for achieving privacy of communication and the use of digital signatures for certifying the validity, integrity, and origin of a message, document, or program. Rather than offering a how-to on configuring Web browsers and e-mail programs, the author provides a guide to the principles and elementary mathematics underlying modern cryptography, giving readers a look under the hood for security techniques and the reasons they are thought to be secure.

PHILIP N. KLEIN is Professor of Computer Science at Brown University. He was a recipient of the National Science Foundation's Presidential Young Investigator Award, and he has received multiple research grants from the National Science Foundation. He has been made an ACM Fellow in recognition of his contributions to research on graph algorithms. He is a recipient of Brown University's Award for Excellence in Teaching in the Sciences.

A CRYPTOGRAPHY PRIMER
Secrets and Promises

PHILIP N. KLEIN

Brown University, Providence, Rhode Island

CAMBRIDGE
UNIVERSITY PRESS

CAMBRIDGE
UNIVERSITY PRESS

Shaftesbury Road, Cambridge CB2 8EA, United Kingdom

One Liberty Plaza, 20th Floor, New York, NY 10006, USA

477 Williamstown Road, Port Melbourne, VIC 3207, Australia

314–321, 3rd Floor, Plot 3, Splendor Forum, Jasola District Centre, New Delhi – 110025, India

103 Penang Road, #05–06/07, Visioncrest Commercial, Singapore 238467

Cambridge University Press is part of Cambridge University Press & Assessment, a department of the University of Cambridge.

We share the University's mission to contribute to society through the pursuit of education, learning and research at the highest international levels of excellence.

www.cambridge.org
Information on this title: www.cambridge.org/9781107017887

© Philip N. Klein 2014

First published 2014

A catalogue record for this publication is available from the British Library

Library of Congress Cataloging-in-Publication data
Klein, Philip N., author.
A cryptography primer : secrets and promises / Philip N. Klein,
Brown University, Providence, Rhode Island.
pages cm
Includes bibliographical references and index.
ISBN 978-1-107-01788-7 (hardback) – ISBN 978-1-107-60345-5 (paperback)
1. Computer security.   2. Data encryption (Computer science)   3. Digital signatures.
4. Telecommunication–Safety measures.   I. Title.
QA76.9.A25K557   2014
005.8′2–dc23   2013046193

ISBN   978-1-107-01788-7   Hardback
ISBN   978-1-107-60345-5   Paperback

Contents

Preface

In his autobiography, *A Mathematician's Apology*, the number theorist and pacifist G. H. Hardy wrote

> ... both Gauss and lesser mathematicians may be justified in rejoicing that there is one science [number theory] at any rate ... whose very remoteness from ordinary human activities should keep it gentle and clean.

Hardy's book was published in 1940, toward the end of his career. If he had postponed his judgment for another 30 years, he might have come to a different conclusion, for number theory became the basis for an important technology long associated with war: cryptography, the use of secret codes.

Cryptography has been in use for at least several thousand years. It is listed in the *Kama Sutra* as one of the 64 arts to be mastered by women. One well-known elementary cryptosystem is attributed to Julius Caesar. Numerous anecdotes attest to the importance of cryptography in war and diplomacy over the years – and to that of cryptanalysis, the cracking of codes. For example, Britain's interception and deciphering of the Zimmerman telegram, a message from Germany's foreign minister to the government of Mexico (via the ambassador), helped speed the United States' entry into World War I, for the message promised Texas, New Mexico, and Arizona to Mexico in return for its help against the United States. Cryptanalysis has played a role in somewhat less momentous events as well; the following is excerpted from the autobiography of Casanova (1757):

> Five or six weeks later, she asked me if I had deciphered the manuscript .... I told her that I had.
> "Without the key, sir, excuse me if I believe the thing impossible."
> "Do you wish me to name your key, madame?" "If you please."

I then told her the key-word which belonged to no language, and I saw her surprise. She told me that it was impossible, for she believed herself the only possessor of that word which she kept in her memory and which she had never written down.

I could have told her the truth – that the same calculation which had served me for deciphering the manuscript had enabled me to learn the word – but on a caprice it struck me to tell her that a genie had revealed it to me. This false disclosure fettered Madame d'Urfe to me. That day I became the master of her soul, and I abused my power.

In the Information Age, however, cryptography's greatest contribution may be to commerce. Banks have long used cryptography to protect the security of electronic transfers. Geographically distributed corporations have used cryptography to protect their communication from industrial espionage. Perhaps the most exciting applications, however, involve securing communication between parties that have no previous connection and have therefore had no opportunity to agree on a key in advance. As commerce on the Internet grows, such applications will become ever more prevalent. Fortunately, technologies such as exponential key exchange and public-key cryptography exist to make such applications possible.

Public-key cryptography, proposed by Diffie and Hellman in 1976, is the idea of having two separate keys, a public key for encryption of a message and a secret key for its decryption; a party can privately construct the two keys and then make the encryption key public without thereby revealing the decryption key. Subsequently, anyone can encrypt messages intended for the creator of the keys, but only the creator can decrypt. The first realization of this idea was due to Rivest, Shamir, and Adleman in 1978. The extent to which their scheme has captured the popular imagination is reflected by the following excerpt from a Harlequin romance, *Sunward Journey:*

"I'm really not into computers, Jay. I don't know much. I do know the key to the code was the product of two long prime numbers, each about a hundred digits, right?"

"Yes, that's correct. It's called the RSA cryptosystem."

"Right, for Rivest, Shamir, and Adleman from MIT. That much I know. I also understand that even using a sophisticated computer to decipher the code it would take forever," she recalled. "Something like three point eight billion years for a two-hundred-digit key, right?" "That's exactly correct. All of the stolen information was apparently tapped from the phone lines running from the company offices to your house. Supposedly no one except Mike had the decoding key, and no one could figure it out unless he passed it along, but there has to be a bug in that logic somewhere," he said, loosening his dark green silk tie. "Vee, it's much warmer than I thought. Would you mind if I removed my jacket?"

"Of course not. You're so formal," she remarked ....

As our heroine, Vee, states, RSA is based on properties of the product of two prime numbers. Thus it harnesses Hardy's favorite area of "pure" mathematics, number theory. The basis of this cryptosystem (like most) is the dichotomy between easy and hard. Creating the public and secret keys is roughly as easy as selecting and multiplying the two hundred-digit prime numbers. As Vee asserts, cracking the system (using currently known methods) requires an exorbitant amount of time; it seems to require one to determine the two prime numbers from their product, a problem called integer factorization. Though progress on this problem continues, known algorithms (recipes) to solve it are not fast enough to seriously threaten the security of RSA – not yet, anyway. To quote a man known more for marketing skill than expertise in number theory,

> Because both the system's privacy and the security of digital money depend on encryption, a breakthrough in mathematics or computer science that defeats the cryptographic system could be a disaster. The obvious mathematical breakthrough would be development of an easy way to factor large prime numbers. – Bill Gates, *The Road Ahead*, first edition, p. 265

(To factor a number is to determine the prime numbers that when multiplied together form the number; if a number is prime then factoring yields just the number itself.)

But RSA has uses other than encryption. As Diffie and Hellman realized, the flip side of public-key cryptography is digital signatures. Using a method such as RSA, the creator of the two keys can construct a *signature* for a document, a number derived from the document in such a way that anyone who knows the public key can verify the signature is consistent with that document. Furthermore, only someone who knows the secret key can construct a valid signature for a given document, so a valid signature associated with a document is strong evidence that the creator of the keys was responsible for producing the signature. If someone tampers with the document, the signature will no longer bear the same mathematical relation to the document, so the document will be deemed invalid. Digital signatures can thus be used to authenticate messages sent over the Internet, guarding against undetected tampering and forged messages. They can be used for creating unforgeable certificates, such as an electronic version of a credit card or passport. They can also be used to detect unauthorized changes to a computer program, such as the introduction of a virus.

Other technologies for computer security have been developed, including methods for securely authenticating a party (the secure analogue of reciting a phone card number or credit card number or mother's maiden name over the telephone), methods for committing to a document without revealing it (the secure analogue of a sealed envelope), and methods for time-stamping a document (the secure analogue of mailing oneself a letter in order to get it postmarked).

The technology of cryptography rests on the science of computation in that it crucially relies on the fundamental premise of that science, the dichotomy between computationally easy problems and computationally difficult problems: codes should be easy to decrypt if you know the key, hard if you don't. Cryptography is thus a concrete realization of this intellectual pursuit.

In order to expose a broader audience to the excitement of this fun, increasingly important, and intellectually challenging field, I have developed a course, "Secrets and Promises: An Introduction to Digital Security." I have written this book for that course. The word "secrets" in the title refers to the use of cryptography for achieving privacy of communication; the word "promises" refers to the use of digital signatures for certifying the validity, integrity, and origin of a message, document, or program. This text is intended as a gentle introduction to the principles and elementary mathematics underlying modern cryptography. It is not a practical, "how-to" text; it will not instruct readers in the use of present-day computer programs (such as web browsers and e-mail programs) that employ digital security. Such programs are forever evolving; moreover, they will be successful in the marketplace only if using them does not depend on knowledge of the underlying security techniques. In this text, we will look under the hood; we will study the security techniques and the reasons they are thought to be secure.

For some of the fundamental cryptographic schemes, such as AES and SHA, the details are rather unenlightening. In this text, we will omit detailed discussion of these schemes. The roles these schemes play will instead be filled by schemes based on elementary number theory. These number-theoretic schemes are a bit too slow to be used in practice, but they are considered secure and they fit better into the curriculum of this text. Thus we make some sacrifice in adherence to practice in order to achieve greater uniformity and readability. Those readers hungry for details on AES, etc., can easily find them in other texts.

Acknowledgments

Many thanks to Sarah Finney, Peter Galea, Kevin Ingersoll, and Mark Weaver, who have helped shape the course on which this text is based. Thanks also to the National Science Foundation, which helped to sponsor the course's development. Thanks to Michael Yanagisawa, who helped in proofreading. Thanks, finally, to Alice, Bob, Eve, and the other characters that frequent the literature of modern cryptography.

1

Introduction

1.1. Encryption and decryption

The most familiar use of cryptography is in concealing the contents of a message or a document. A *cryptosystem* is a system to achieve this. It consists of two parts: an encryption method and a decryption method. The unaltered, readable form of the message or document is called *plaintext* or *cleartext*. The altered, presumably unreadable form is called *cyphertext*. (Another name for *cryptosystem* is *cypher*, also spelled *cipher*.)

$$\text{plaintext} \quad \xrightarrow{\text{encryption}} \quad \text{cyphertext}$$
$$+ \text{key} \quad \xleftarrow[\text{decryption}]{} \quad + \text{key}$$

Encryption is the process of obtaining cyphertext from plaintext. The encryption method requires two inputs: the plaintext and the secret key. Similarly, the decryption requires two inputs: the cyphertext and the key – and outputs the plaintext.

In a traditional cryptosystem, the same key is used to encrypt and to decrypt. Such a system is called a *symmetric-key cryptosystem*. If Alice is to send an encrypted message to Bob, they both have to know the key. (This is to be distinguished from a *public-key cryptosystem*, in which one key is used for encrypting and another for decrypting. We discuss public-key cryptosystems later.) If Alice and Bob wish to keep the contents of the message a secret, the key had better be a secret, for any eavesdropper who knows the key and intercepts the cyphertext can determine the plaintext.

We are assuming here that every prospective eavesdropper knows the encryption and decryption methods; this assumption is discussed in Section 1.4. We continue to make this assumption throughout this text; it is methodologically fundamental to the modern study of cryptography. To

1

amplify, *always assume that every prospective adversary knows all the details of every cryptographic system you employ.*

Cryptanalysis is the process of trying to crack a cryptosystem; an eavesdropper would employ methods of cryptanalysis to try to figure out the contents of Alice's message to Bob. In Section 1.6, we briefly describe some of the different kinds of attacks an eavesdropper might mount, but details of cryptanalysis are beyond the scope of this text.

1.2. Channels, secure and insecure

We use a variety of communication media: telephone networks, the radio waves, TV cable networks, local computer network, the Internet, print media. Banks use one network to connect their automatic teller machines to central computers and another network to execute electronic funds transfer. Paging services use a combination of cable and radio. Some communication between satellite and earth makes use of microwaves. I often use my computer's memory to communicate between my present self and my future self. When I use a telephone, even before my voice reaches the handset, the sound passes through the air. In fact, in the act of dialing I communicate with the phone system.

We would like to apply the concepts of digital security to any and all of these communication media. To this end, we use a single, generic term, *channel*, to abstract away the differences between them. A *channel* is a medium for communication between two parties. (I like to think of a string connecting two tin cans.)

Of course, most communication media enable communication between more than two parties. However, for most purposes the notion of a channel that connects two parties is sufficient; if more parties are involved, we simply invoke the presence of more channels.

Whether one considers a particular communication medium (e.g., the phone network) to be secure or insecure depends on one's point of view. For example, we ordinarily think of the phone network as being reasonably secure, but many hundreds of government wiretap and bug orders are approved each year, and each order leads to surveillance of a couple of thousand conversations on average.

For the purposes of studying cryptography, we shall simply declare whether we consider a channel to be secure or insecure. The channel is insecure if it is possible for a third party (an eavesdropper) to intercept (listen in on) a message passing through the channel. In some cases, it may even be possible for the eavesdropper to alter the message as it goes from sender to receiver.

A *secure* channel is a channel that is immune to eavesdropping or tampering. Cryptography is much more interesting, of course, when applied to an insecure channel. Fortunately (or unfortunately, depending on your point of view), insecure channels abound in real life. In the remainder of this section, we outline some of the characteristics of three communication media that make them insecure. These are intended as examples; readers can no doubt find sources of insecurity in other communication media, including those mentioned at the beginning of this section.

1.2.1. The Internet

Today, the most obvious applications of cryptography involve the Internet, for three reasons. First, the Internet is in part composed of computers, and computers are great at cryptography. Second, the Internet is the perfect medium for facilitating spontaneous communication between large numbers of previously unacquainted parties. Third and most important, the very structure of the Internet renders it needful of security mechanisms. Each computer in the Internet is *directly* connected to very few other computers. When you send a message from the computer in your bedroom in Rhode Island to your parents' computer in California, your message travels through many intermediate computers. Each of these intermediate computers is expected to do its best to forward your message to another computer closer to the message's destination, and there are mechanisms to check whether the message eventually finds its way there. However, nothing in the system prevents an intermediate computer from storing a copy of the message it forwards, or altering the message before forwarding it. A rogue computer could even fail to forward your message but return a message to your computer indicating that your original message did get through.

(The situation is not as dire as this description would make it seem; the route taken by your message is frequently unpredictable, and often your message is split into pieces and the pieces sent along different routes. Most of the intermediate computers encountered are not likely to be rogues.)

A worse situation arises during *remote log-in*. If you have an account on a computer in California, you can use your computer in Rhode Island to log in to the computer in California, by using a program called "telnet." The Californian computer will, of course, send a message requesting your password. When you provide it, the password travels through all the intermediate computers between Rhode Island and California. Any one of these intermediate computers could store the address of the Californian computer, your user name, and your password, and later gain access to your account. There is evidence that tens of thousands of passwords have been obtained in this way by rogue computers.

Now that the Internet is widely used for commercial purposes, the dangers have proliferated. Suppose you use your Web browser to obtain up-to-date stock information before making a business decision; it is possible (though not all that probable) that your business rival has set up a computer to substitute his own, falsified data for the stock information you sought. Suppose you decide to download your favorite computer-game company's latest demonstration program. It is possible that some rogue computer has intercepted your browser's request and responded with an altered, virus-infected version of the program you requested. Finally, suppose you are viewing the Web page of an online bookseller. They provide a way to encrypt your credit card number, and you send it to them. The page you were viewing might not be the bookseller after all; it might be a front put up by a rogue computer.

1.2.2. Local area networks

One need not communicate with locales as far apart as California and Rhode Island to encounter security risks. Your *local area network* (which connects your computer to servers that store programs and provide mail service) may not be secure; rogue computers connected to that network may be able to intercept your communication (using a program called a "packet-sniffer") and even inject altered data.

1.2.3. Cellular phones

Of course, cellular phone communication takes place over the airwaves and thus can be intercepted, as Newt Gingrich, Speaker of the House, found out in January 1997. It is not only one's conversations that are at risk; when a call is initiated, the cellular phone transmits an account number to be charged. The cellular telecommunications industry suffered an estimated 450 million dollars in fraud losses in 1995,[1] much of that due to cellphone "cloning": bandits would intercept the account numbers and install the numbers on other cell phones, thereby "cloning" the original phones. Calls on the new cell phones would be charged to the old ones.

The cellular telecommunications industry is taking steps to prevent fraud, incorporating security features. Old communications standards die hard,

---

[1] Source: Bell Atlantic, http://www.ba.com/nr/95/may/freddie.html

however. Moreover, the security features introduced are not necessarily full-proof, as discussed in Section 1.3.

One need not even be using one's cellular phone to be vulnerable to a security risk. As a cellular phone travels, it registers its change of location with the system; this transmission can be intercepted and used to help determine the location of the phone (and of its owner). The FBI has requested standards to mandate that every cellular phone could provide police with the location of phone users.[2]

1.3. Security through obscurity

Consider the following:

- During World War II, the U.S. military hired Navajo Indians to handle secure communications in the Pacific theater. No cryptography was used to ensure the privacy of the communication; it was considered secure enough that the communication took place in the Navajo language. As far as we know, the security of this system was never broken.
- In Edgar Allan Poe's "The Purloined Letter," the eponymous epistle was "hidden" in an obvious place – and remained hidden from the police (though not from the story's protagonist).
- An imaginary colleague of mine at another university wants to make the rough draft of the midterm available to his TAs to review – so he leaves the midterm in a public folder but names it "systemstats," thinking nobody would bother to look at this folder.

These are examples of "security through obscurity." The idea is that one can achieve security by keeping a particular mechanism secret. The concept (though not the name) has a long history – a history with many failures. When one party (often a government) relies on a secret method for achieving security, another determined party can often exploit espionage, luck, and/or long hours of work to determine the method being used. Examples from the twentieth century include the Polish-British success in cracking the German enigma cryptosystem and the American success in cracking the Japanese encryption machine 07-shiki O-bun In-ji-ki.[3]

Developers of security methods are still seeking security through obscurity. A recent example, dating from March 1997, concerns a cryptosystem used in

---

[2] The Communications Assistance for Law Enforcement Act. Source: http://www.epic.org/privacy/wiretap/

[3] Kahn, *The Codebreakers*.

digital cellular telephony to encrypt numbers punched in by a user of a cellular phone, for example, for dialing. The details of the cryptosystem were supposed to be known only to industry engineers, but were leaked and published on the Web. Some researchers subsequently showed that the system is much less secure than desirable.[4]

Relying on obscurity to achieve security is a mistake. This is especially the case in an age when digital security is ubiquitous, when it is used primarily for commerce, when most secure communication takes place between parties that have had no prior contact. The *usefulness* of security mechanisms in commerce depends on their being widely distributed. Under these circumstances, it is wildly optimistic to assume that details of a security method will not fall into the hands of someone capable of finding and exploiting any security hole.

1.4. The alternative: The Kerckhoffs Doctrine

Given that obscurity is not a reliable source of security, what alternatives do we have? After all, *something* must be secret.

The answer, or at least part of it, was first articulated in 1881 by an impressive polymath who was at that time a professor of German in a Paris university.[5] He was born Jean-Guillaume-Hubert-Victor-François-Alexandre-Auguste Kerckhoffs von Nieuwenhof but later shortened his name to Auguste Kerckhoffs. He spent much of his working life teaching English and German but on occasion also taught Italian, Latin, Greek, history, and mathematics. The subjects of books he authored include grammar, the origins of German drama, the relation of art to religion, and, of course, cryptography. In *La Cryptographie militaire*, he recognized that cryptosystems then being proposed were far from secure:

> ... I am stupefied to see our scholars and our professors teach and recommend for wartime use systems of which the most inexperienced cryptanalyst would certainly find the key in less than all hour's time.

Kerckhoffs recognized that the spurious claims of security, often based on such misleading calculations as the number of centuries required to systematically try all keys, helped foster ignorance and gullibility about cryptography:

> ... it may... be believed that the immoderate assertions of certain authors, no less than the complete absence of any serious work on the art of solving secret writing,

---

[4] http://www.counterpane.com/cmea.html
[5] This material is from Kahn, *The Codebreakers*.

have largely contributed to give currency to the most erroneous ideas about the value of our systems of cryptography.

Kerckhoffs thus realized that the security of a cryptosystem cannot generally be established by its developer via pure reasoning but must be subjected to the rigors of attack by independent crypt analysts.[6] He inferred the principle that we shall call the Kerckhoffs Doctrine: *The security of a cryptosystem should depend only on the secrecy of the key used, not on the secrecy of the system itself.*

The Kerckhoffs Doctrine requires you to assume that every prospective eavesdropper and hacker has access to all the details of the cryptosystem you are using. This is a pessimistic assumption but, especially in cases where there is a great deal at stake, one that is frequently warranted. As Schreier writes, "...one would assume that the CIA does not make a habit of telling Mossad [the Israeli secret service] about is cryptographic algorithms, but Mossad probably finds out anyway." The Kerckhoffs Doctrine is particularly applicable for security systems intended to be used by many people (such as the security systems in Web browsers), for all these people must be granted at least implicit access to the details of the systems – and your adversary is likely to be among these people.

The Kerckhoffs Doctrine is appealing but would be empty if no cryptosystem existed that could satisfy the Doctrine's stringent requirement. What hope do we have of coming up with a system so secure that a determined adversary with full knowledge of the system could not crack it? As Edgar Allan Poe wrote in his celebrated story *The Gold-Bug*, "it may well be doubted whether human ingenuity can construct an enigma of the kind which human ingenuity may not, by proper application, resolve." As I hope to show in this text, there are good reasons to believe that secure cryptosystems do in fact exist.

1.5. A taxonomy of cryptography

Although *cryptography* in a narrow sense means the study of secret writing (*encryption*), it has come to be a generic term for a variety of technologies arising in digital security. In studying cryptography, it is useful to make distinctions among different conceptual levels. For now, the following five categories suffice:

1. Vague security goals
2. Formal security goals

---

[6] We shall see an exception to this rule when we study perfect secrecy.

3. Protocols
4. Cryptographic building blocks
5. Realizations of these building blocks

Vague security goals are the most abstract elements in cryptography, and are what motivate all the rest. "I want my communications with so-and-so to be private." "I want an unforgeable document." "I want to ensure that any modifications to the computer program are detectable." Though the point of cryptography is to serve such goals, it is hard to verify whether such goals have been met because the terms are so vague. To ensure that communication will be private, for example, we must guarantee that no eavesdropper learns the contents of the communication. What information and what resources are available to a prospective eavesdropper? What actions are available to her? Whether or not it is possible for the eavesdropper to learn the content of communication depends crucially on the answers to these questions.

For more precision of language and more specificity, we must turn to *formal security goals*. A formal security goal states that an adversary pursuing a particular kind of attack and possessing certain resources (e.g., time, memory, computational power) cannot succeed. We discuss different kinds of attacks in Section 1.6. We can delve deeper into formal security goals only after we have discussed probability theory and computational complexity.

A cryptographic *protocol* is a set of rules for communicating between multiple parties to achieve some cryptographic goal. For example, we discuss later how two parties can communicate to agree securely on a secret key; the protocol to achieve this is called *exponential key agreement*. One can think of encrypt-send-receive-decrypt as a very simple protocol: one party encrypts the plaintext and sends it to the other party, who decrypts it. Another simple protocol, used for *authentication*, is logging in to a computer: a person sends a message requesting access to the computer; the computer responds by asking for the password; the person sends back the password; the computer sends back a message granting access. We will study more sophisticated authentication protocols as well.

Protocols are built on *cryptographic building blocks*. The most familiar kind of cryptographic building block is a cryptosystem, but in this text we discuss several other kinds as well, including one-way functions, message digest functions, and digital signature systems. One commonly associates with each cryptographic building block an informal or formal security goal.

It is often useful to distinguish between conceptual building blocks and particular *realizations of these building blocks*. Thus, for example, there are many different cryptosystems but they all fill essentially the same role in achieving security goals. Part of the power of modern cryptography derives from researchers having identified and characterized useful cryptographic building blocks at an abstract level.

Abstraction enables the developer of a cryptographic protocol to achieve much greater generality. For example, if the protocol makes use of a cryptosystem, the developer need not spell out precisely which cryptosystem to use ("encrypt a message using the cryptosystem DES…"), only what security goals the cryptosystem must satisfy. This generality in turn makes the protocol more robust: if someday the use of DES is abolished (as some argue it should be today), the protocol can simply use another cryptosystem, such as IDEA.

The generality afforded by abstraction is not merely a tool of researchers. Protocols such as SSL, which is built into current Web browsers and is invoked for most secure Web interactions, is designed to make use of any of a large variety of realizations of the fundamental cryptographic building blocks.

For the most conceptually novel building blocks, such as public-key encryption and digital signatures, we will describe the precise realization used in practice. However, as mentioned in the preface, for some other building blocks – symmetric-key encryption, one-way functions, and message digest functions – we do not describe in detail the realizations typically used in practice. Those details are not all that enlightening, and the design principles that gave rise to them are beyond the scope of this text. In their place we describe other realizations for the same cryptographic building blocks. The realizations we describe, if used correctly, can be just as secure as the practical realizations. We will be careful to inform readers when our descriptions diverge from practice.

1.6. Attacks on cryptosystems

Let us make this slightly more concrete by focusing on the most familiar cryptographic tool, encryption. Suppose Alice needs to send a private message to Bob, and therefore encrypts the message using a secret key known only to her and Bob. The goal here of our eavesdropper, Eve, is to violate privacy of communication. In the worst case, this could mean that Eve is able to read precisely what has been communicated. Typically this entails her knowing the secret key used for encryption. (Recall Casanova's story from the preface.) However, it would still be a violation of Alice and Bob's privacy if by observing the cyphertext Eve were to gain some information about the contents of the message without learning it precisely and wholly. Even such a partial break in a cryptosystems can have serious implications (e.g., the VENONA project, which we shall study later).

The phrase "gain some information" is pretty vague. We do not have the technical apparatus, at least at this stage in the text, to formalize that notion. Let us proceed, nevertheless, to consider what sort of information Eve might use in cracking the security of the cryptosystem. Traditionally, a distinction is made between four types of attacks. In increasing order of power, they are:

- Cyphertext-only attack
- Known plaintext attack
- Chosen plaintext attack
- Chosen cyphertext attack

Suppose that after intercepting one or more cyphertexts sent from Alice to Bob, Eve could analyze these cyphertexts and gain some information about the corresponding plaintexts. We say in this case that Eve has used a *cyphertext-only* attack.

Suppose Eve intercepts a cyphertext for which she happens to already know the plaintext. She might be able to analyze the relation between plaintext and cyphertext to determine some information about the key. Such information could help her to decrypt other cyphertexts encrypted with the same key. We say in this case that Eve has used a *known plaintext attack*. In a more general version of this attack, she might be able to obtain and make use of *many* plaintext–cyphertext pairs.

Now we consider a more active attack by Eve. Suppose she is able to choose plaintexts for Alice to encrypt. Alice innocently goes along, encrypting plaintexts of Eve's choosing. It is conceivably useful to Eve to have plaintext–cyphertext pairs for which she has chosen the plaintext. What we have described is called a *chosen plaintext* attack. As an historical example, the U.S. ambassador to Japan during World War II reported that "one of the high officials of the Japanese Government wanted to send a secret message to our Government which they did not want the Japanese military to see and in passing this message on they asked me to please put it in our most secret code. I said of course I would do so."[7]

In a slight twist on her attack, Eve might be sufficiently friendly with Bob to get him to decrypt putative cyphertexts of her choosing. That is, Eve makes up alleged cyphertexts without having any idea of the corresponding plaintext, and convinces Bob to provide her the decryptions of these alleged cyphertexts. This is called a *chosen cyphertext* attack, and it can in fact be useful, for example,

---

[7] Kahn, p. 495.

if the cyphertexts Eve makes up are somehow related to some real cyphertexts she wants to crack. There is an attack of this form on the RSA cryptosystem.

1.7. Problems

1. For each of the following communication scenarios, give a brief argument for or against the security of that channel. Note: this does not need to be technical. We don't have specific answers in mind for this question.
   (a) Placing a credit-card order over the telephone
   (b) Withdrawing cash from an ATM
   (c) Paying a utility bill by mail
   (d) Sending an e-mail to your professor
2. Your eternal archnemesis, Eve, has joined the teaching staff of a cryptography class in which you are enrolled. Given this fact, explain, in your own words, what kinds of risks you are taking by running software provided for use in the course. Again, your answer need not be technical.

2

Modular Arithmetic

2.1. The Caesar cypher

Julius Caesar, we are told (by a contemporary writer, Suetonius[1]), made use of a cryptosystem in which the plaintext letter A was replaced by D in the cyphertext, B was replaced by E, and so on. The last three letters of the alphabet would be replaced, respectively, by the first three letters of the alphabet. Here's an example of encryption:

plaintext	V	E	N	I		V	I	D	I		V	I	C	I
numeric	21	4	13	8		21	8	3	8		21	8	2	8
+ 3	24	7	16	11		24	11	6	11		24	11	5	11
cyphertext	Y	H	Q	L		Y	L	G	L		Y	L	F	L

To describe the *Caesar cypher* mathematically, we represent each letter of the alphabet by an integer between 0 and 25: 0 for A, 1 for B, ..., 25 for Z. Then encrypting a plaintext element between 0 (A) and 22 (W) consists simply of adding three. What about encrypting 23 (X) or 24 (Y) or 25 (Z)? For each of these, we encrypt by adding 3 but in an unusual way – once we get past 25, we start over at 0. Thus to encrypt 24, we add 1, obtaining 25, then add 1 again, obtaining not 26 but 0, then add 1 once more, obtaining 1. Similarly, to encrypt 25, we add 1, obtaining not 26 but 0, then add 1 a couple more times, obtaining 2.

Decrypting works the same way but by *subtracting* 3 instead of adding 3 – with the proviso that subtracting three from 0 yields 23, subtracting three from 1 yields 24, and subtracting three from 2 yields 25.

---

[1] Source: Kahn, Chapter 2.

2.2. The number *circle*

Just as we can visualize ordinary addition and subtraction using a number line, we can visualize this kind of addition and subtraction using a number *circle*:

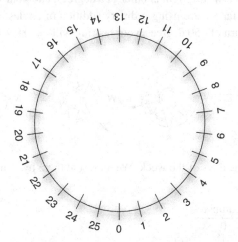

The number circle makes it clear that, as you move clockwise past 25, you return to 0; if you move counterclockwise from 0, you reach 25.

Addition using this number circle is called *modulo 26 addition*. In the world of modulo 26, there are exactly 26 numbers. On the number line we have indicated them as 0 through 25. The number 26 is called the *modulus*. Of course, we often work with other moduli, as in the examples to follow.

2.3. Modular arithmetic in daily life

You have undoubtedly seen modular addition before, though perhaps not by that name. For example, consider the face of a clock:

Suppose it is 9 o'clock, and you want to know what time it will be in 6 hours. You would use modulo 12 arithmetic: 9 plus 6 is 3 (modulo 12).

In dealing with compass bearings and angles, the modulus to use is 360. Suppose you are heading due north; your bearing is 0 degrees. Next you turn 110 degrees right; your new bearing is 110 degrees (which is roughly east–southeast). Now turn right another 120 degrees, and your bearing will be 230 degrees. So far we are using ordinary addition of angles. However, after one more right turn of 150 degrees, your bearing will be ~~380~~ 20 degrees.

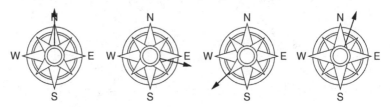

Or consider the days of the week. We represent them by numbers as shown here:

Day	Number
Sunday	0
Monday	1
Tuesday	2
Wednesday	3
Thursday	4
Friday	5
Saturday	6

In this context, it is helpful to use 7 as the modulus. Suppose today is Thursday, which is represented by 4. What day will it be in 5 days? We add 5 to 4, obtaining ~~9~~ 2, so it will be Tuesday. What day will it be in 13 days? We add 13 to 4, obtaining ~~17~~ 3, so it will be Wednesday. What day will it be in 700 days? Note that 700 days is exactly 100 weeks, so it will be the same as today, Thursday. This last example illustrates that adding multiples of 7 makes no change. Adding 7 has the same effect as adding 14, which has the same effect as adding 21, or adding 0, or subtracting seven.

2.4. Congruences

Mathematicians formalize modular arithmetic using the idea of *modular congruences*. Two integers are said to be *congruent* with respect to a given modulus if they differ by a multiple of that modulus. For example, if the modulus is 7, then 3, 10, and 17 are congruent. A statement that two expressions are congruent is called a *congruence*.

2.4.1. Congruences modulo 7

Let's use 7 as our modulus. Two integers are *congruent* modulo 7 if they differ by a multiple of 7. For example, 4 is congruent to 11 (which is 4 + 7) and to 18 (which is 4 + 2 · 7) and even to –3 (which is 4 + (−1) · 7). The mathematical notation for writing a congruence is similar to the mathematical notation for writing an equation: whereas the equality symbol has two horizontal bars ("="), the congruence symbol has three ("≡"). For example, we write the congruence

$$1 \equiv 8 \pmod 7$$

to state that 1 is congruent (modulo 7) to 8. Note that the notation calls for us to specify the modulus in parentheses together with the word "mod," short for "modulo."

Here are more modulo 7 examples. Readers can verify that the numbers are indeed congruent by checking that the difference between them is a multiple of 7:

$$2 \equiv 30 \pmod 7$$
$$-9 \equiv -2 \pmod 7$$
$$-20 \equiv 8 \pmod 7$$
$$7 \equiv 0 \pmod 7$$
$$14 \equiv 0 \pmod 7$$

Of course, if two numbers are *equal*, their difference is 0, which is a multiple of 7 (zero times 7 is zero). This shows that any true *equation* corresponds to a true congruence. For example, since 4 + 5 = 9, the congruence

$$4 + 5 \equiv 9 \pmod 7$$

is true.

Finally, we sometimes get tired of writing "modulo 7" over and over. If (as often occurs) we are doing lots of arithmetic with the same modulus, we can just say up front that the modulus is, for example, 7, and then not mention it again! Thus it is okay to say "1 is congruent to 8" or write "1 ≡ 8" if everybody already knows the modulus is 7.

2.5. Another example: Congruences modulo 10

One of my favorite moduli is 10 because it is easy to determine congruence when using this modulus. Consider, for example, the integer 314,159. This number can be written as

$$314, 159 = 31, 415 \times 10 + 9$$

This equation shows that 314,159 differs from 9 by a multiple of 10. Thus the following congruence is true:

$$314, 159 \equiv 9 \quad (\text{mod } 10)$$

Similarly, any positive integer is congruent (modulo 10) to its ones digit because the rest of the integer is a multiple of 10.

It follows that two positive integers are congruent (modulo 10) if their ones digits match.

2.6. Substituting using congruences

You probably know how to simplify an equation by replacing a subexpression by something *equal* to the subexpression. For example, because $12 + 4$ is equal to 16, we can rewrite the equation

$$(12 + 4) \cdot 2 = x + 1$$

as

$$16 \cdot 2 = x + 1$$

When working with congruences, we can similarly replace any subexpression involving $+$, $-$, or $\times$ by a congruent subexpression. Here is an example. Suppose the following mod 7 congruence is true:

$$(12 + 4) \cdot 2 \equiv x + 1 \quad (\text{mod } 7)$$

Because $12 + 4$ is congruent (mod 7) to 2, we infer the mod 7 congruence

$$2 \cdot 2 \equiv x + 1 \quad (\text{mod } 7)$$

The idea of substitution in congruences is so important that we state it as a principle:

The Substitution Principle of Congruences For any true modular congruence, replacing any subexpression with a congruent subexpression yields another true modular congruence.

2.6.1. *Using substitution to simplify adding together many numbers*

Substitution can make modular calculations easier. Let us start with the congruence

$$5 + 6 + 3 + 4 + 5 + 6 \equiv x \quad (\text{mod } 7)$$

Now $5 + 6$ is 11, and 11 is congruent to 4, so we can replace the subexpression $5 + 6$ by 4, obtaining

$$4 + 3 + 4 + 5 + 6 \equiv x \quad (\text{mod } 7)$$

Continuing in this manner, $4 + 3$ is 7, and 7 is congruent to 0, so we can replace the subexpression $4 + 3$ by 0:

$$0 + 4 + 5 + 6 \equiv x \quad (\text{mod } 7)$$

Because $0 + 4 + 5$ is 9, which is congruent to 2, we replace $0 + 4 + 5$ by 2:

$$2 + 6 \equiv x \quad (\text{mod } 7)$$

Finally, $2 + 6$ is 8, which is congruent to 1, so we obtain

$$1 \equiv x \quad (\text{mod } 7)$$

2.6.2. *Using substitution to simplify multiplying together many numbers*

This technique is even more useful when multiplications involved because it can be used to keep the numbers from getting too big. Let us start with the congruence

$$5 \cdot 6 \cdot 3 \cdot 4 \cdot 5 \cdot 6 \equiv x \quad (\text{mod } 7)$$

Now $5 \cdot 6$ is 30, and $30 = 4 \cdot 7 + 2$, so 30 is congruent to 2. We may therefore replace the subexpression $5 \cdot 6$ by 2:

$$2 \cdot 3 \cdot 4 \cdot 5 \cdot 6 \equiv x \quad (\text{mod } 7)$$

Continuing, $2 \cdot 3$ is 6, so we obtain

$$6 \cdot 4 \cdot 5 \cdot 6 \equiv x \quad (\text{mod } 7)$$

Because $6 \cdot 4$ is 24, which is congruent to 3, we can replace $6 \cdot 4$ by 3, obtaining

$$3 \cdot 5 \cdot 6 \equiv x \quad (\text{mod } 7)$$

Because $3 \cdot 5$ is 15, which is congruent to 1, we can replace $3 \cdot 5$ by 1, obtaining

$$1 \cdot 6 \equiv x \quad (\text{mod } 7)$$

which in turn implies

$$6 \equiv x \pmod 7$$

In the above derivation, we never had to multiple numbers greater than 6 because after each multiplication we replaced the product with a congruent number less than the modulus. This technique is essential when one must deal with congruences involving multiplying thousands of integers. As we will see, such congruences arise in cryptography.

2.6.3. Casting out nines

Mod-nine arithmetic is the basis for a useful trick for checking ordinary arithmetic. Suppose you have made a calculation involving multiplications and additions, but you're not sure you got the right answer. For example, is the following equation true?

$$5837 \cdot 48 + 42,090 \stackrel{?}{=} 327,066$$

As explained in Section 2.4.1, if an equation is true, then, for any modulus, the corresponding congruence holds. In particular, using 9 as the modulus, if the above equation were true, then the following congruence would also be true:

$$5837 \cdot 48 + 42,090 \stackrel{?}{\equiv} 327,066 \pmod 9$$

To simplify this congruence, let's write out the number 5937 in terms of its decimal digits:

$$5837 = 5 \cdot 10^3 + 8 \cdot 10^2 + 3 \cdot 10 + 7$$

- First consider $3 \cdot 10$. Modulo 9, 10 is congruent to 1, so $3 \cdot 10$ is congruent to $3 \cdot 1$, which is just 3.
- Next, consider $8 \cdot 10^2$. Now 10^2 is $10 \cdot 10$. Because 10 is congruent to 1, $10 \cdot 10$ is congruent to $1 \cdot 1$, which is 1, so $8 \cdot 10^2$ is congruent to $8 \cdot 1$, which is 8.
- Finally, consider $5 \cdot 10^3$. By the same reasoning, 10^3 is congruent to 1, so $5 \cdot 10^3$ is congruent to 5.

Putting these statements together, $5 \cdot 10^3 + 8 \cdot 10^2 + 3 \cdot 10 + 7$ is congruent to $5 + 9 + 3 + 7$. *That is, the number 5837 is congruent to the sum of its digits.*

This process applies to any positive number: Because $10, 10^2, 10^3$ and higher powers of 10 are all congruent to 1 (modulo 9), any positive integer is congruent (modulo 9) to the sum of its digits.

We can use this idea repeatedly. We have seen that 5837 is congruent to
$5 + 8 + 3 + 7$, which is 23. The number 23 in turn is congruent to the sum of
its digits, $2 + 3$, which is 5. Thus 5837 is congruent to 5.

What about $5837 \cdot 48$? The number 48 is congruent to the sum of its digits,
$4 + 8$, which is 12. The number 12 is congruent to the sum of its digits, which
is 3. Thus, using substitution, $5837 \cdot 48$ is congruent to $5 \cdot 3$, which is 15, and
15 is congruent to $1 + 5$, which is 6.

What about $5837 \cdot 48 + 42,090$? We have seen that $5837 \cdot 48$ is congruent
to 6. Using the sum-of-digits rule, we infer that 42,090 is congruent to $4 + 2 +$
$0 + 9 + 0$, which is $6 + 9$. Because we are working modulo 9, we automatically
know that 9 is congruent to zero, so $6 + 9$ is congruent to 6. (Any time we see
the digit 9, we can leave it out of our sum; any time we see some digits that
add up to 9, such as 2 and 7, we can leave them out. This is the reason this
technique is called "casting out nines.)"

We know that $5837 \cdot 48$ is congruent to 6, and that 42,090 is congruent to 6.
Therefore, by substitution, $5837 \cdot 48 + 42,090$ is congruent to $6 \cdot 6$, which is
36. Since the digits of 36 sum to 9, it is congruent to zero.

Our goal was to check the congruence

$$5837 \cdot 48 + 42,090 \stackrel{?}{\equiv} 327,066 \quad (\mathrm{mod}\ 9)$$

The left-hand side is congruent to zero. What about the right-hand side? One
way to simplify the right-hand side is simply to add up the digits, obtaining
24, and then add up the digits of 24, obtaining 6. A quicker way is to observe
that the digits 2 and 7 sum to 9, and the digits 3 and 6 sum to 9, and the only
remaining digits are 0 and 6, which sum to 6. In either case, we have shown
that the right-hand side is congruent to 6. We earlier showed that the left-hand
side was congruent to zero. Because zero is *not* congruent to 6, the congruence
is *not* true. This shows that the original equation $5837 \cdot 48 + 42,090 \stackrel{?}{=} 327,066$
was not true.

We have illustrated a way of checking the truth of an ordinary arithmetic equation involving $+$ and $\times$. This method of checking is much easier
and less error-prone than carrying out all the additions and multiplications
by hand. The method won't catch all errors. In particular, if the original
equation is false but the left-hand side and the right-hand side differ by
a multiple of 9, the corresponding congruence will be true. However, the
method does catch errors most of the time. More important for our purposes, it is another illustration of the usefulness of substitution in dealing with
congruences.

2.7. Representatives and remainder

Consider a representative democracy in which every person has exactly one representative. We will mimic this idea in modular arithmetic. For a particular modulus m, we define the *representatives* to be the integers $0, 1, 2, \ldots, m - 1$. The reason for this definition is the following theorem:

Representative Theorem: Every integer is congruent modulo m to exactly one of the integers $0, 1, 2, \ldots, m - 1$.

For example, modulo 7, every integer is congruent to exactly one of the integers $0, 1, 2, 3, 4, 5, 6$.

2.7.1. Quotient and remainder

The theorem is based on the following fundamental result in number theory:
Quotient-and-Remainder Theorem: For every integer b and every positive integer m, there is exactly one integer q and exactly one integer r among $0, 1, 2, \ldots, m - 1$ such that

$$b = qm + r \qquad (2.1)$$

Examples:

- Let $b = 25$ and let $m = 7$. Then Eq. (2.1) is satisfied by $q = 3$ and $r = 4$. (That is, $25 = 3 \cdot 7 + 4$.)
- Let $b = 62$ and let $m = 7$. Then Eq. (2.1) is satisfied by $q = 8$ and $r = 4$. (That is, $62 = 8 \cdot 7 + 6$.)
- Let $b = 99$ and let $m = 12$. Then Eq. (2.1) is satisfied by $q = 8$ and $r = 3$. (That is, $99 = 8 \cdot 12 + 3$.)

As the examples suggest, r is the *remainder* when b is divided by m, and q is the *quotient*. Finding the remainder is an arithmetic operation just like addition and multiplication. In the spirit of the $+$ and the $\times$ operators, therefore, we define a operator, rem, to signify taking the remainder. We define b rem m to denote the value of r described in the Quotient-and-Remainder Theorem. (The name *rem* is short for *remainder*.)

Examples:

- 25 rem 7 is 4.
- 62 rem 7 is also 4.
- 99 rem 12 is 3.

What has rem to do with modular arithmetic? The value of b rem m is exactly b's mod m representative!

- $r = b$ rem m is one of the integers $0, 1, 2, \ldots, m - 1$, which shows that it is a representative.
- The equation $b = qm + r$ shows that b and r differ by a multiple of m, which shows that b is congruent to r (mod m).

2.7.2. Using rem *to check whether two numbers are congruent*

One use of rem is in finding out whether two numbers a and b are congruent modulo m.

Showing congruence

We can use the following argument.

> Suppose a and b have the same mod-m representative. It follows that they are both congruent (mod m) to that representative, and hence congruent to each other.

In Mathese, we write

> if a rem $m = b$ rem m then $a \equiv b$ (mod m).

Is 30 congruent (mod 7) to 51? To find out, we compute the mod 7 representatives of 30 and 51. The remainder of 30 divided by 7 is 2, so 2 is the representative of 30. The remainder of 51 divided by 7 is 2, so 2 is also the representative of 51. Therefore 30 is congruent to 2 and 51 is congruent to 2, so 30 and 51 are congruent to each other.

Showing non-congruence

We see that we can use *rem* to show that two integers are congruent to each other. Can we use *rem* to show that two integers are *not* congruent to each other?

We use the following argument.

> Suppose that a and b are congruent (mod m). Because a is congruent to its representative and b is congruent to a, it follows that b is congruent to a's representative. Because b is congruent to exactly one integer among $0, 1, 2, \ldots, m - 1$, namely its representative, b's representative must be a's representative.

In Mathese, we write

if $a \equiv b$ (mod m) then a rem $m = b$ rem m.

It follows that if a's representative is *not* the same as b's representative, then a and b *cannot* be congruent.

Is 40 congruent (mod 7) to 73? We compute the representatives of 40 and 73. The remainder of 40 divided by 7 is 5, so 5 is the representative of 40. The remainder of 73 divided by 7 is 3, so 3 is the representative of 73. Because 40 and 73 have different representatives, they are *not* congruent to each other.

2.7.3. Using rem *to simplify modular congruences*

In Sections 2.6.1 and 2.6.2, we used the Substitution Principle of Congruences to help in checking complicated congruences. In each step we replaced a subexpression with a congruent subexpression. By adopting the rule that we always replace a subexpression with its representative, we can ensure that our intermediate results don't get too big – in particular, that the intermediate results are always less than the modulus.

Suppose we want to solve the congruence

$$12 \cdot 11 \cdot 10 \cdot 9 \cdot 8 \cdot 7 \equiv x \quad (\text{mod } 13)$$

Instead of multiplying out the numbers on the left-hand side, we carry out one multiplication at a time, always replacing the product with its mod-13 representative:

$12 \cdot 11$ is 132, and the remainder of 132 divided by 13 is 2, so we replace $12 \cdot 11$ with 2, and we replace the original congruence with

$$2 \cdot 10 \cdot 9 \cdot 8 \cdot 7 \equiv x \quad (\text{mod } 13)$$

$2 \cdot 10$ is 20, and the remainder of 20 divided by 13 is 7, so we replace $2 \cdot 10$ with 7, obtaining the congruence

$$7 \cdot 9 \cdot 8 \cdot 7 \equiv x \quad (\text{mod } 13)$$

Continuing in this way, we replace $7 \cdot 9$ with $7 \cdot 9$ rem 13, which is 11, obtaining

$$11 \cdot 8 \cdot 7 \equiv x \quad (\text{mod } 13)$$

Then we replace $11 \cdot 8$ with $11 \cdot 8$ rem 13, which is 10, yielding

$$10 \cdot 7 \equiv x \quad (\text{mod } 13)$$

We replace $10 \cdot 7$ with $10 \cdot 7$ rem 13, which is 5. We finally obtain

$$5 \equiv x \quad (\text{mod } 13)$$

so $x = 5$ is a solution.

2.7.4. Using rem to simplify equations involving rem

Suppose you are asked to compute

$$12 \cdot 11 \cdot 10 \cdot 9 \cdot 8 \cdot 7 \cdot 6 \text{ rem } 13$$

We know that the result of computing the remainder is a mod-13 representative. Using the fact that

if $a \equiv b \pmod{m}$ then a rem $m = b$ rem m

we see that we will get the same answer if we replace $12 \cdot 11 \cdot 10 \cdot 9 \cdot 8 \cdot 7$ with any congruent subexpression. The calculations in Section 2.7.3 show that

$$12 \cdot 11 \cdot 10 \cdot 9 \cdot 8 \cdot 7 \equiv 5 \quad (\text{mod } 13)$$

so we need only compute

$$5 \cdot 6 \text{ rem } 13$$

and it is easy to calculate the value of this expression, 4.

2.7.5. Representatives of negative integers

We have said that b rem m is the remainder when b is divided by m. However, what we mean by *remainder* is specified by the Quotient-and-Remainder Theorem, in which the remainder is defined to be a nonnegative integer. This could conflict with the reader's intuition about the remainder when b is a negative number. For example, one might expect -15 rem 7 to be -1 (-15 divided by 7 is -2 with remainder -1), but we need the answer to be a mod-7 representative. The representative that is congruent to -1 is 6, so we define -15 rem 7 to be 6. Similarly, -3 rem 7 is 4, and -25 rem 7 is 3.

2.8. Problems

1. Explain your answers to the following questions. Today is Wednesday.
   (a) What day will it be in 7 days?
   (b) In 67 days what day will it be?
   (c) If a government proposal were passed to lengthen the weekend by sticking in an extra day after Saturday, what day would it be 67 days from now?

2. Examine the number $4.51283512835128351283\ldots$

   What is the 295th digit after the decimal point in this number? Explain how you got your answer.

3. A simple two-person game is as follows. There is a pile of pennies between you and your opponent. The two of you take turns taking either one, two, or three pennies. Your goal is to force your opponent to take the last penny. Try out the game with a friend, then answer the following questions.

   (a) Fill in the missing entries of the following table.

Number of pennies	best move
1	lose
2	take 1
3	take 2
4	take 3
5	?
6	?
7	?
8	?
9	?
10	?

   (b) Let n be the number of pennies in the table. It is your turn. How many pennies should you take? Give the answer in terms of n.

   (c) Repeat Problem a. for the variant of the game in which each player can take one, two, three, or four pennies:

Number of pennies	Best move
1	lose
2	take 1
3	take 2
4	take 3
5	take 4
6	?
7	?
8	?
9	?
10	?

   (d) Repeat Problem b. for the variant.

4. For each of the following congruences, find the solution for x. Your solution should be a representative (one of $0, 1, 2, \ldots, m - 1$ where m is the modulus).

(a) $x \equiv 4 + 3 \pmod 8$

(b) $x \equiv 7 + 34 \pmod 4$

(c) $13 + 22 \equiv x \pmod{13}$

(d) $6 - 7 \equiv x \pmod{88}$

(e) $x \equiv 9 - 19 \pmod 7$

5. Find the (representative) solution for x.

(a) $12 + 4 + 7 + 12 + 17 \equiv x \pmod{12}$

(b) $7 + x \equiv 2 \pmod 3$

(c) $x \equiv 16 + 2 \pmod 8$

(d) $x \equiv 57 \cdot 73 \pmod{17}$

(e) $x \equiv 3 \cdot (87 - 5) \pmod 7$

(f) $x \equiv (-5) - (-11) \pmod{10}$

6. Compute the following

(a) $16 + 2 \text{ rem } 8$

(b) $57 \cdot 73 \text{ rem } 17$

(c) $3 \cdot (87 - 5) \text{ rem } 7$

(d) $(-5) - (-11) \text{ rem } 10$

3

The Addition Cypher, an Insecure Block Cypher

The Caesar cypher is easy to crack. The most straightforward attack makes use of the fact that the number of possible keys is so small. Suppose that Eve were to intercept the following cyphertext, encrypted using the Caesar cypher on a 27-symbol alphabet consisting of space, A, ..., Z ..

UMTSJENXEYFUUJI

The first thing she would do is to enumerate the 27 possible keys, and, for each, find the corresponding cyphertext. She would obtain:

UMTSJENXEYFUU JI	VNUTKFOYFZGVVKJ
WOVULGPZG HWWLK	XPWVMHQ HAIXXML
YQXWNIRAIBJYYNM	ZRYXOJSBJCKZZON
PHONE IS TAPPED	SZYPKTCKDL PO
AT ZQLUDLEMAAQP	BUA RMVEMFNBBRQ
CVBASNWFNGOCCSR	DWCBTOXGOHPDDTS
EXDCUPYHPIQEEUT	FYEDVQZIQJRFFVU
GZFEWR JRKSGGWV	H GFXSAKSLTHHXW
IAHGYTBLTMUIIYX	JBIHZU CMUNV J JZY
KCJI VDNVOWKK Z	LDKJ AWEOWPXLLA
MELKBXFPXQYMMBA	NFMLCYGQYRZNNCB
OGNMDZHRZS OODC	QIPOFAJTAUBQQFE
RJQPGBKUBVCRRGF	SKRQHCLVCWDSSHG

If she had reason to believe that the plaintext might be in English, it would not be difficult for her to guess it from the list of possible plaintexts above.

This example demonstrates that a cryptosystem is insecure if the number of possible keys is too small. The converse, however, is not true: a cryptosystem with many possible keys is not necessarily a secure cryptosystem. In this chapter, we outline a simple cryptosystem, a generalization of the Caesar cypher we call the addition cypher. We use this cryptosystem to illustrate the notion of a block cypher and to illustrate several simple cryptanalytic attacks.

3.1. The addition cypher

Let's start with the Caesar cypher, and try to repair its most obvious flaw, the small number of possible keys. The encryption method is modular addition, where the modulus is the size of the alphabet, and there is a possible key for each representative. Let us drastically increase the modulus, for this will increase the number of possible keys. For example, let's use a modulus of 1000000000000 (i.e., 10^{12}). Imagine the Caesar cypher done with an alien alphabet that consists of 10^{12} letters. The key will be a representative with respect to this modulus, namely any number from 0 to 999999999999. To encrypt a single letter of the alien alphabet, one adds the corresponding number to the key; the result, reduced to a representative (a nonnegative integer less than 10^{12}), is one letter of cyphertext.

We would like to use this system with plaintexts written in our own puny alphabet. Here is one way to do this: we use a number from 0 to 999999999999 to represent a sequence of six symbols. Each two digits of the number represents one symbol. Two digits allow us to represent any of 100 symbols, which is plenty to represent the space, all lowercase letters and uppercase numbers, the digits, and various typographic symbols. For example, the sequence "we try" would be represented by the number 230500201825. Suppose Alice wished to encrypt this plaintext using the key 620487370109. The resulting cyphertext, obtained by adding 230500201825 and 620487370109 modulo 10^{12}, would be 850987571934.

3.2. Block cyphers

Of course, a cryptosystem that allowed only six-symbol plaintexts would be of limited utility. How could Alice use the addition cypher to encrypt a plaintext consisting of, say, 50 symbols? The generic name for a scheme is *block cypher*. The basic encryption method is called *block encryption*, and the size of the plaintext that block encryption can handle is called the *block size*, and can be measured by the number of digits. For example, the system described in Section 3.1 has a block size of 12 digits, and its block encryption method consists in adding the plaintext and the key modulo 10^{12}.

The simplest scheme for obtaining a block cypher is called ECB mode, and is illustrated in Figure 3.1 (ECB stands for "Electronic Code Book"). Alice

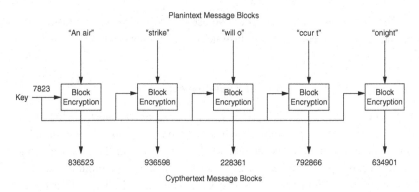

Figure 3.1. A diagram illustrating ECB mode.

breaks her plaintext into blocks. The first block consists of the first 12 digits,
the second block consists of the next 12 digits, and so on. There are five such
blocks in this case; the last block has some extra zeroes to "pad" it out to
the right length. Next, Alice encrypts each block separately. The same key is
used for all the blocks. Finally, she takes her cyphertext to be the sequence of
encryptions of the blocks.

Let's look at a small example. Say Alice were using a version of the addition
cypher that allows only two digits of plaintext, that is, the plaintext is a number
between 0 and 99. The key is also a number between 0 and 99. The cyphertext
is obtained by adding the plaintext to the key, doing the arithmetic mod 100, so
the cyphertext is a number between 0 and 99. Suppose Alice wants to encrypt
a plaintext consisting of 16 digits, say 3057205711654928. Say her key is 11.
She breaks her plaintext into eight blocks:

$$30\ 57\ 20\ 57\ 11\ 65\ 49\ 28$$

Next, she encrypts each block separately, using 11 as her key. The encryption of 30 is 41, the encryption of 57 is 68, and so on. Thus she gets eight
blocks of cyphertext:

$$41\ 68\ 31\ 68\ 22\ 77\ 60\ 39$$

She puts these blocks together to obtain her cyphertext, 4168316822776039,
which she sends to Bob. To decrypt this cyphertext, Bob similarly breaks the
cyphertext into the same eight blocks, and decrypts each block in turn.

Note that the above scheme is essentially a Caesar cypher (albeit with a
modulus of 100 instead of 26). If the plaintext has predictable properties, the
cyphertex will have related properties. For example, if the block 05 represents "e" and therefore occurs often in the plaintext, the block 16 occurs often

in the cyphertext. If Eve knows that this kind of cypher is being used but doesn't know the key, she could analyze a long cyphertext and plausibly hope to learn something about the key and thus about the plaintext. To resist this sort of attack, a cryptographer designing a block cypher should ensure that the block size is large enough that such patterns rarely occur, say 20 digits or more.

3.3. Attacks on the addition cypher

Even with a huge block size, the addition cypher when used in ECB mode is insecure. We discuss some attacks on it.

3.3.1. Known-plaintext attack

Let's suppose Alice and Bob have previously agreed on a secret key, and Alice sends Bob a long message encrypted with the addition cypher using a block size of, say, 20 digits. Suppose further that Eve intercepts the cyphertex and that she happens to know or suspect that Alice starts all her messages to Bob with the symbols "Dear Bob." Thus Eve knows both the plaintext and the cyphertext of the first block. She uses the block-encryption equation

$$cyph = plain + key \operatorname{rem} 10^{20}$$

to calculate the key:

$$key = cyph - plain \operatorname{rem} 10^{20}$$

With the key safely in hand, Eve can now decrypt all the rest of the blocks of the cyphertext.

We see that if Eve knows a single block of plaintext and the corresponding cyphertext, she can figure out the key.

Suppose next that Eve does not know with certainty how Alice's message starts: she knows 20 (or even 10,000) different ways that Alice's message is likely to begin. She can use the same procedure as above with each of these possible first blocks of plaintext, obtaining a corresponding number of possible keys. She then tries each of these keys in turn, using it to decrypt the entire message. For each *spurious key* (a possible key that turns out to not be correct), Eve probably gets gibberish as the corresponding plaintext. For the correct key, Eve gets a meaningful plaintext.

It is possible that for some of the spurious keys, the corresponding plaintext is not gibberish. However, if the message is long enough, this is exceedingly unlikely. Furthermore, even if Eve simply manages to narrow down to two or three the possible plaintexts Alice sent, she will have succeeded in violating Alice's privacy and thus in breaking the scheme's security. Note that in this latter attack, Eve uses her prior knowledge of the sort of messages Alice might send. She uses her fairly precise knowledge of the first block of the plaintext (the same trick would work on any other particular block, e.g., the last), and she uses her knowledge that the entire message is likely to be in English.

3.3.2. Cyphertext-only attack

In some cases, Eve need not have any idea of the precise plaintext in order to obtain useful information from the cyphertext. She can instead exploit general knowledge of the nature of the message.

For example, suppose that the beginning of every month Alice sends Bob a message consisting of the amount Bob should spend that month on advertising Alice's product. The message is encrypted with the 20-digit addition cypher, using the same key every month. (It's a safe assumption that the plaintext is smaller than 10^{20}, even if Alice works for Bill.) Eve is Alice's competitor, and wants to know how Alice's advertising budget changes from month to month. Suppose Eve intercepts the January and February cyphertexts. She writes down the following two equations.

$$Jan.\ cyph. = Jan.\ plain + key\ \text{rem}\ 10^{20}$$

$$Feb.\ cyph. = Feb.\ plain + key\ \text{rem}\ 10^{20}$$

and notices that by subtracting one equation from the other, she obtains

$$Jan.\ cyph. - Feb.\ cyph. \equiv Jan.\ plain - Feb.\ plain(mod\ 10^{20})$$

Because Eve knows the cyphertexts from January and February, she can subtract modulo 10^{20} to obtain the mod 10^{20} difference between the January plaintext and the February plaintext. That is, she obtains the mod-10^{20} representative of the difference between January's advertising budget and February's.

The true difference is either the mod-10^{20} representative of the difference (if the true difference is positive) or else it is the mod-10^{20} representative minus 10^{20} (if the true difference is negative). It should not be hard for Eve to figure out which is the true difference. (All this will perhaps be more clear to a reader who tries out an example with smaller numbers, e.g., budgets around 10 or 15 and a modulus of, say, 50.)

3.4. Attacks on any block cypher that uses ECB mode

So far we have seen attacks that use specific properties of the addition cypher. However, any block cypher used in ECB mode has security weaknesses. For example, note that if the same block of plaintext occurs in different messages, the corresponding cyphertext blocks are identical. Suppose Alice is sending encrypted buy-and-sell orders to her broker Bob. Eve intercepts these cypher-texts, and waits to see what actions Bob then takes in the market. If some of the same blocks recur in later cyphertexts, Eve can guess at some of the orders, and can herself act in anticipation of Bob's actions.

Because of the security weaknesses of ECB mode, it is rarely used. We will discuss other, somewhat more secure block-cypher modes later.

3.5. Problems

1. Suppose you are Eve, the eavesdropper. You intercept the following symbol of cyphertext: "L." You know that it was encrypted using the Caesar cypher, but you don't know the key. Enumerating all the keys, determine all the possible decryptions.
2. Now consider the use of the encryption function as the basis for a block cypher. That is, encrypt (or decrypt) each symbol of the plaintext separately. Suppose you, again Eve, intercept the following cyphertext which you know has been encrypted with a block cypher based on the Caesar cypher. Given that the cleartext is English text, how might you go about decrypting this message?

   KYVVCVGYREKZJREXIP.

3. Suppose now that you have learned that the key is 17. What is the plaintext?
4. Assume you are using an alphabet that contains only four charac-ters/symbols (Say, "A," "B," "C," and "D").
   (a) How many different Caesar cyphers can be used with this alphabet? (i.e., how large is the keyspace?)
   (b) How many different possible substitution keys exist for this alphabet?

4

Functions

4.1. The basics

A *two-place relation* is a way of pairing up members of one set with members of another set. We can use a diagram to represent a relation; there is an arrow for each pair, going from the first item in the pair to the second. Thus all the figures in this chapter, starting with Figure 4.1, represent two-place relations.

If there is an arrow $x \longrightarrow y$ in the relation, we say that "x maps to y" and that "y is the image of x" under the relation. Thus in the relation depicted by Figure 4.1, the elements 1, 4, and 5 all map to 96, 1 also maps to 94, the element 2 maps to 100, and finally 3 maps to 99. Another way to say the same thing is that 96 is the image of 1 and is also the image of 4 and of 5, and so forth.

A *one-input function* is a special kind of two-place relation, one for which each item in the first set has exactly one outgoing arrow, that is, each such item maps to exactly one element of the second set. Thus Figure 4.2 represents a one-input function, but Figure 4.1 does not. In fact, there are two ways in which the relation depicted in Figure 4.1 fails to be a function. There are elements of the first set (namely 1) that maps to two things, and there are elements (namely 6) that map to no elements.

The first set is called the *domain* of the function, and the second set is called the *codomain*. Thus the domain of the function depicted in Figure 4.2 is the set $\{0, 1, 2, 3, 4, 5\}$, and the codomain is $\{0, 1, 2, 4, 6, 12, 20\}$. Note that for that function, not every element of the codomain is the image of something (i.e. has an arrow pointing to it). That is, there are elements of the codomain (namely 2 and 4) that have no incoming arrows. This is fine; it does not violate the definition of a function. (Later we'll talk about functions in which every element of the codomain has at least one incoming arrow; such a function is said to be *onto*.) The set of elements of the codomain that are images of elements of the

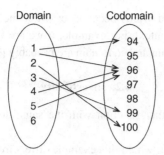

Figure 4.1. A two-place relation that is not a function.

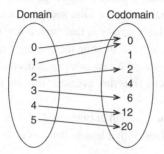

Figure 4.2. An example of a function with the domain $\{0, 1, 2, 3, 4, 5\}$.

domain constitute the *range* of the function. Thus a function's range is a subset of its codomain. The range of the function in Figure 4.2 is $\{0, 2, 6, 12, 20\}$.

Think of the elements of the domain as *inputs* to the function. The corresponding output is the thing that the input points to. We refer to the set of outputs as the range. Again, the main rule for functions is that **there must be a single arrow coming out of each element of the domain.**

For some functions, there is a nice mathematical rule that tells you, for each input, how to calculate the corresponding output. For example, for the function depicted in Figure 4.2, the rule is

$$x \mapsto x \cdot (x - 1)$$

To use this, suppose you want to calculate the output corresponding to 3. Copy the formula on the right of the $\mapsto$ but replace x with 3. The resulting formula tells you the output corresponding to 3 (namely $3 \cdot 2$, which is 6).

However, one must keep two points in mind.

1. The rule does not completely specify the function; the domain and codomain must also be specified.
2. Not all functions have nice rules to describe them.

Rule 1 is not followed strictly because very often the domain and codomain are obvious from the context. For example, if we are working with numbers modulo 7 then the domain and codomain are probably $\{0, 1, 2, 3, 4, 5, 6\}$.

4.2. Invertibility

Figure 4.3 depicts another function with the same domain as the previous example.

One important way in which this example differs from the previous one is that in this example each element of the codomain is the image of precisely one element of the domain. It is easy to recognize such functions from their diagrams. (This is the main reason we use such diagrams.)

The significance of this property is that such a function is *invertible*. That is, if you turn the arrows around, treating the old range as a domain and the old domain as a codomain, you get a new function. This new function is called the *inverse* of the old function. Thus the inverse of the function in Figure 4.3 is the function depicted in Figure 4.4.

Try doing that with the function of Figure 4.2. You get the two-place relation depicted in Figure 4.5. Notice that some elements of the new domain (e.g., 0)

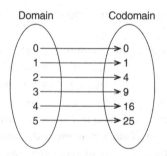

Figure 4.3. A function with the same domain as that of Figure 4.2.

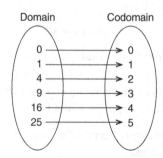

Figure 4.4. The inverse of the function of Figure 4.3.

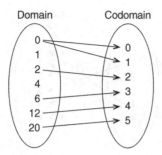

Figure 4.5. An attempt to represent the inverse of the function of Figure 4.2. This relation is not a function.

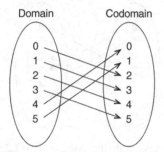

Figure 4.6. The function with the domain $\{0, 1, 2, 3, 4, 5\}$ and the rule $x \mapsto x + 2$ rem 6.

have multiple arrows coming out of them. Thus the diagram does not represent a function.

Back to invertible functions and their inverse. Take a guess – what is the inverse of the function depicted in Figure 4.4? Right, the inverse is the function of Figure 4.3. The inverse of the inverse of a function is the original function. (Nothing deep there; you turn arrows around once and then turn them around again. They end up back where they started.)

When we know a rule for an invertible function, we can sometimes use the rule to help make sense of the inverse. For example, a rule for the function depicted in Figure 4.3 is $x \mapsto x \cdot x$. That is, the rule says to square the input in order to get the output. What operation is the reverse (formally, the *inverse*) of squaring? The square root! Thus the rule for the inverse function, the function of Figure 4.4, is $y \mapsto \sqrt{y}$, (We used a different variable, y, in the rule; this doesn't really have any significance.)

In Figure 4.6 is depicted a function. One rule for describing this function is $x \mapsto x + 2$ rem 6. The function maps 0 to 2, 1 to 3, and so on – so the inverse

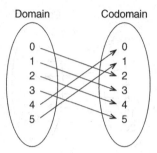

Figure 4.7. The inverse of the function in Figure 4.6.

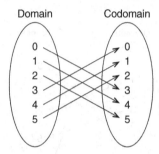

Figure 4.8. The function with the domain $\{0,1,2,3,4,5\}$ and the rule $x \mapsto x+3$ rem 6.

should map 2 to 0, 3 to 1, and so on. The inverse is shown in Figure 4.7. One rule describing the inverse is $y \mapsto y+4$ rem 6.

Here's another example. In Figure 4.8 is depicted a function. One could describe the function using the rule $x \mapsto x+3$ rem 6.

What is the inverse of this function? The function maps 0 to 3, 1 to 4, 2 to 5,.... so the inverse should map 3 to 0, 4 to 1, 5 to 2,.... Wait a minute! The function is its own inverse!

4.2.1. One-to-one and onto

We have said that a function is invertible if every element of the codomain is the image of precisely one element of the domain. Let's break down that condition into two conditions, one-to-one and onto:

- A function is *one-to-one* if each element of the codomain is the image of **at most** one element of the domain.
- A function is *onto* if each element of the codomain is the image of **at least** one element of the domain.

These terms are used for explaining why a function is not invertible. A function that is not one-to-one is not invertible. Also a function that is not onto is not invertible. (A function that is neither one-to-one nor onto is definitely not invertible.)

On the other hand, these are the only possible reasons a function fails to be invertible.

Invertibility Principle: An invertible function is a function that is both one-to-one and onto.

4.3. Functions from modular arithmetic

4.3.1. Modular addition and additive inverse

The function depicted in Figure 4.6 is described by the rule $x \mapsto x + 2$ rem 6. Its inverse, depicted in Figure 4.7, can be described by the rule $y \mapsto y + 4$ rem 6.

What's the 4 doing in the latter rule? What does it have to do with the 2 in the former rule? The answer lies in the congruence

$$2 + 4 \equiv 0 \quad (\text{mod } 6) \tag{4.1}$$

This congruence shows that four plays the role of negative 2 in mod-6 addition. Indeed, the mod-6 representative of negative 2 is 4. In virtue of Congruence 4.1, we say that 4 is the mod-6 *additive inverse* of two (and vice versa).

More generally, if a and b are integers satisfying the congruence

$$a + b \equiv 0 \quad (\text{mod } m)$$

we say that a and b are mod-m *additive inverses* of each other.

Consider the function with domain $\{0, 1, 2, \ldots, m - 1\}$ described by the rule $x \mapsto x + a$ rem m. If b is the mod-m additive inverse of a then the inverse function is described by the rule $y \mapsto y + b$ rem m (as can be proved using the Subsitution Principle).

4.3.2. Computing a mod-m additive inverse

Does every integer a have a mod-m additive inverse? If so, how can we find it? Here ordinary arithmetic can help. Setting $b = -a$ satisfies the equation $a + b = 0$ so certainly $a + b \equiv 0$ (mod m). Thus $-a$ is a mod-m additive inverse of a. The mod-m representative of $-a$ is $m-a$. Thus $b = m-a$ is also a mod-m additive inverse of a (and has the advantage of being a representative).

4.3.3. Modular multiplication and multiplicative inverse

The situation with multiplication is similar but a bit more complicated. Consider the function with domain $\{1, 2, 3, \ldots, 6\}$ and the rule $x \mapsto x \cdot 2$ rem 7. This function is depicted in Figure 4.9.

This function maps 1 to 2, 2 to 4, 3 to 6, and so on. Its inverse, therefore, maps 2 to 1, 4 to 2, 6 to 3, and so on. The inverse is shown in Figure 4.10.

The inverse function can be described by the function $y \mapsto y \cdot 4$ rem 7. This is a consequence of the congruence

$$2 \cdot 4 \equiv 1 \quad (\text{mod } 7) \tag{4.2}$$

This congruence shows that 4 plays the role of $\frac{1}{2}$ in mod-7 multiplication. In virtue of Congruence 4.2, we say that four is the mod-7 *multiplicative inverse* of two (and vice versa).

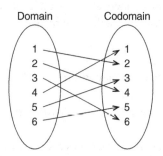

Figure 4.9. The function with domain $\{1, 2, 3, 4, 5, 6\}$ and the rule $x \mapsto x \cdot 2$ rem 7.

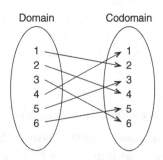

Figure 4.10. The inverse of the function shown in Figure 4.9.

More generally, if a and b are integers satisfying the congruence

$$a \cdot b \equiv 1 \pmod{m}$$

we say that a and b are mod-m *multiplicative inverses* of each other.

In this case, the function described by $x \mapsto x \cdot a$ rem m and $y \mapsto y \cdot b$ rem m are inverses of each other. (This can be shown using the Substitution Principle.)

Multiplicative inverses will play a crucial role in several of the cryptographic schemes we will study in later chapters.

4.3.4. Finding mod-7 multiplicative inverses the simple way

To find other mod-7 multiplicative inverses, we write down the mod-7 multiplication table for mod-7 representatives:

	0	1	2	3	4	5	6
0	0	0	0	0	0	0	0
1	0	1	2	3	4	5	6
2	0	2	4	6	1	3	5
3	0	3	6	2	5	1	4
4	0	4	1	5	2	6	3
5	0	5	4	3	2	1	2
6	0	6	5	4	3	2	1

Searching this table for ones, we see that

- 1 is its own multiplicative inverse ($1 \cdot 1 \equiv 1 \pmod{7}$),
- 2 and 4 are multiplicative inverses of each other ($2 \cdot 4 \equiv 1 \pmod{7}$),
- 3 and 5 are multiplicative inverses of each other ($3 \cdot 5 \equiv 1 \pmod{7}$), and
- 6 is its own multiplicative inverse ($6 \cdot 6 \equiv 1 \pmod{7}$).

Clearly this method for finding multiplicative inverses can be used with any modulus m: just write down the mod-m multiplication table for all mod-m representatives, and search it for ones. In Chapter 8, we study a method that is more practical when the modulus m is large.

4.3.5. Multiplicative inverses don't always exist

Now consider the function with domain $\{1, 2, 3, 4, 5\}$ and rule $x \mapsto x \cdot 2$. This function is depicted in Figure 4.11. Note that $3 \cdot 2 = 0$ so, to use that rule, we must include 0 in the codomain. The function is not invertible. (It is neither one-to-one nor onto.) This reflects the fact that 2 has no mod-6 multiplicative inverse.

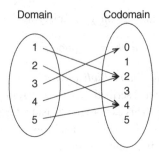

Figure 4.11. The function with domain $\{1, 2, 3, 4, 5\}$ and the rule $x \mapsto x \cdot 2$
rem 7.

To verify this, we write down the mod-6 multiplication table for mod-6
representatives:

	0	1	2	3	4	5
0	0	0	0	0	0	0
1	0	1	2	3	4	5
2	0	2	4	0	2	4
3	0	3	0	3	0	3
4	0	4	2	0	4	2
5	0	5	4	3	2	1

Searching the table for ones, we can see that 1 is its own multiplicative inverse
and 5 is its own multiplicative inverse, but no other representatives have multiplicative inverses. You might find this a bit surprising. After all, in ordinary
arithmetic, for every nonzero number a, there is a number b such that $a \cdot b = 1$.
(Namely, $b = 1/a$.) In Chapter 8, we study the question of when an integer
has a modular multiplicative inverse.

4.4. Function notation

Very often mathematicians refer to functions by name. "Hey, Bob!" No,
actually, mathematicians rarely use "Bob" to refer to a function. Instead, they
typically refer to function by "f". For example, a mathematician might say
"Let f denote the function whose domain is $\{0, 1, 2, 3, 4, 5\}$ and whose rule
is $x \mapsto x^2$ Then f is a one-to-one function." (They use slightly different
terminology, e.g., "rule" is not true Mathese.) Having named the function, a
mathematician can refer to the output corresponding to a specific input.

To denote the output corresponding to 3 (the image of 3), a mathematician writes $f(3)$. Thus the value of $f(3)$ is 9 in this case. It turns out to be remarkably useful to have such concise notation for the output corresponding to a specific input.

There is also notation for the inverse of a function. The inverse of a function named f is denoted f^{-1}. We can refer, for example, to the output of f^{-1} corresponding to input 9 by writing $f^{-1}(9)$, which in this case is 3. Thus 9 maps to 3 under the function f^{-1}.

Clearly mathematicians can't use the same name, "f," to refer to every function they encounter, right? Well, actually, they very often do. The idea is that f is a sort of a temporary name, often used to refer to whatever function is relevant to the current discussion. Thus today f might refer to the function of Figure 4.3 and tomorrow f might refer to a completely different function, even one with a different domain. Of course, good mathematical explanation should make clear which function is meant.

When mathematicians need to refer to more than one function during the same discussion, they resourcefully resort to, yes, the letters g, and h, etc. (not the best example of mathematical creativity). Sometimes they refer to functions by using a combination of a letter and a little number, a subscript. Thus f_1 might denote a function, and f_2 might denote a different one, and f_3 a third one, and so on. There is little chance of running out of names this way.

This subscript scheme can come in handy when one wants to refer to lots of similar functions. For example, consider the "add 3" function. There are lots of other functions of this form: the "add 1" function, the "add 2" function, the "add 4" function, and so on. A mathematician can define all these functions at once by saying "For each number b, let f_b denote the function defined by the rule $x \mapsto x + b$ with the domain $\{0, 1, 2, 3, 4, 5\}$." Now the "add 311" function is denoted f_{311}.

4.5. Uses of functions

Functions provide a terminology and notation that are widely applicable. The key to their flexibility is their abstractness. Here are some non-cryptographic examples (cryptographic examples are given later.) Which of these functions are one-to-one? Which are onto?

- The domain is the set of undergraduates at Brown University; the rule is

$$x \mapsto x\text{'s ID number}$$

- The domain is the set of undergraduates at Brown; the rule is

$$x \mapsto \text{number of hairs on } x\text{'s head}$$

- The domain is the set of staff at Brown; the rule is

$$x \mapsto x\text{'s salary}$$

- The domain is the set of all living people; the rule is

$$x \mapsto x\text{'s mother}$$

- The domain is the set of all commercial stereos; the rule is

$$x \mapsto x\text{'s manufacturer}$$

Of course, one can easily specify a domain and a rule for something that is not really a function. Which of the following describe functions?

- The domain is the set of students at Brown; the rule is

$$x \mapsto x\text{'s roommate}$$

- The domain is the set of students at Brown; the rule is

$$x \mapsto \text{number of semesters } x \text{ has been a student}$$

- The domain is the set of students at Brown; the rule is

$$x \mapsto \text{ the best semester grade } x \text{ has received so far}$$

4.6. A two-input function: The encryption function for the generalized Caesar cypher

The functions that we have considered up to now are all one-input functions (often called *one-place functions*). Some of the concepts (not inverse functions!) carry over readily to two-input functions. Here we consider one useful example, the encryption function for a variant of the Caesar cypher. The two inputs are (1) the plaintext and (2) the key; the output is the cyphertext. We can represent this symbolically by writing

$$f(\textit{plaintext symbol, key}) = \textit{cyphertext symbol}$$

Each of the two inputs should be an element of the set $\{0, 1, 2, 3, \ldots, 25\}$, and the output is an element of this set. The rule for the function is

$$f(plain, key) = plain + key \text{ rem } 26$$

where we have used the names *plain* and *key* instead of, say, x and y, to remind ourselves of the intended purpose of these inputs.

4.7. Specialization: Turning a two-input function into a one-input function

Now suppose two parties, Alice and Bob, have selected a key, say, 17, to be used for their encrypted messages. We can define a new function g to carry out the encryption with that key. The function g has $\{0, 1, 2, 3, \ldots, 25\}$ as its domain and its codomain. It is defined by the rule

$$g(plain) = f(plain, 17)$$

That is, we define g in terms of f. The input to g is the plaintext and the output is the cyphertext. What is the corresponding decryption function? The inverse of g, which we write g^{-1}. Thus g had better be invertible!

Instead of introducing a new name g for the encryption-with-key-17 function, we might instead have used subscripts, referring to the function by $f_{key=17}$. (Same function, different way of naming it.)

This way of getting a one-input function from a two-input function by selecting one of the inputs and sticking to it is sometimes called *specialization*.

We say an encryption function $f(plain, key)$ achieves *unique decryptability* if, for each possible key k, $f_{key=k}(plain)$ is an invertible function.

Note that we could have specialized the function f in another way, by selecting a plaintext symbol (say 2, which stands for "c") instead of a key. That is, we could define the function h by the rule

$$h(key) = f(2, key)$$

The input to h is a key, and the output is the encryption of "c" using that key. The usefulness of this function is less readily apparent than that of g, but we'll see later why it is useful in evaluating the security of a cryptosystem.

Let's see a simple example of specialization. We start with the table describing a two-input function:

y
		1	0
x	1	%	#
	0	&	$

Now we fix the x input to be 1. We now look only at the relevant row of our table:

y
	1	0
x = 1	%	#

This can be interpreted as a function of one input, y. It is shown below:

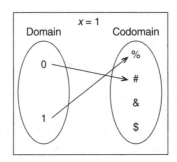

Similarly we can fix the x input to be 0. Here's the function we get:

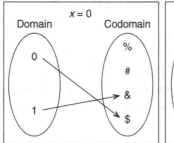
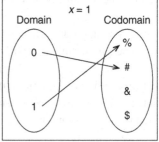

4.8. Problems

1. Remember that the encryption function for the Caesar cypher looks like this: $f(plain, key) = (plain + key)$ rem 26. Let $g(cyph, key)$ be the

decryption function. That is, for a cyphertext $cyph$, $g(cyph, key)$ is the corresponding clear text symbol.

Give the rule for g. $(g(cyph, key) = \ldots?)$

2. For each of the following diagrams, state whether it is or is not a function.

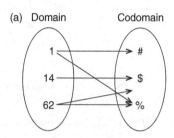

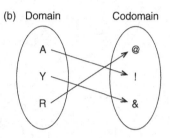

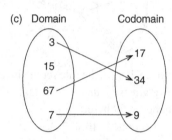

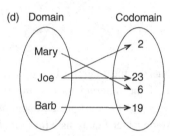

3. For each of the following diagrams, give the rule to which it corresponds.

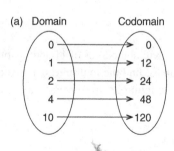

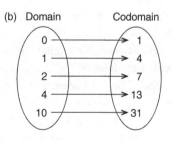

4. Consider the functions depicted in Problem 3.

    (a) Give the rule for the inverse of the function in 3(a).

    (b) Do the same for 3(b).

5. Give a rule for each of the funcitons depicted in the following diagrams:

(a) Domain   Codomain   (b) Domain   Codomain

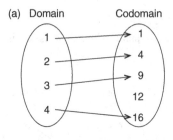 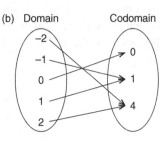

(c) Domain   Codomain   (d) Domain   Codomain

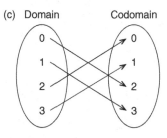 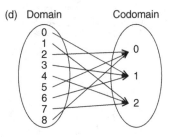

6. Consider the diagrams in Problem 5. For each, give the rule for the inverse or, if the diagram has no inverse, explain why this is the case. (The concepts of one-to-one and onto might be useful here.)

7. We consider functions with domain and codomain $\{0, 1, 2, 3, 4, 5, 6, 7, 8\}$. For each rule below, give the rule for the inverse function.

  (a) $x \mapsto x + 1$ rem 9
  (b) $x \mapsto x + 2$ rem 9
  (c) $x \mapsto x + 3$ rem 9
  (d) $x \mapsto x + 6$ rem 9
  (e) $x \mapsto x + 0$ rem 9

8. Prepare two multiplication tables, one with a modulus of 11 and the other with a modulus of 15. Using your tables, find the multiplicative inverses specified below. For each, if there is no multiplicative inverse, say so and justify your answer.

  (a) mod-11 multiplicative inverse of 5
  (b) mod-15 multiplicative inverse of 4
  (c) mod-15 multiplicative inverse of 5
  (d) mod-11 multiplicative inverse of 11
  (e) mod-15 multiplicative inverse of 3

9. Below we use a table to describe a function of two inputs, x and y. Your job is to take each value for x in turn, plug that value in and thus obtain a one-input function.

	y	
	1	0
x 1	7	13
0	17	5

Fill in the arrows in the following diagram to get the appropriate one-input function diagrams.

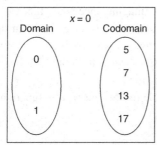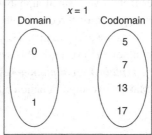

10. We have talked about how a cryptosystem can be described as a two-input function. That is, $f(plain, key) = cyph$. As we saw in Chapter 4, we can hold either the key or the plain input fixed, and make functions with one input for all the possible values of the fixed input.

(a) Consider the following two-input function table that describes a cypher function for encrypting one character out of an alphabet of only three characters. That is, the plaintext and cyphertext can both be either 0, 1, or 2.

	key	
	0	1
0	0	1
plain 1	1	2
2	2	0

Treat the plaintext input as the fixed variable, and fill in the one-input function diagrams provided so that you have a complete description of the function.

Plain = 0		Plain = 1		Plain = 2	
Key	Cyphertext	Key	Cyphertext	Key	Cyphertext
0	0	0	0	0	0
1	1	1	1	1	1
2	2	2	2	2	2

(b) Imagine that you are Eve, and you see a cyphertext that was encrypted and sent by Alice using the encryption function described above. The cyphertext is 2. Given this, one of the plaintexts is not possible. Which one is it?

11. Now we will use a rule to describe a encryption scheme and do the same kind of analysis as in the last problem. To make things less complicated, we are going to stick with schemes that are designed to encrypt a character from a very small alphabet. Imagine once again that we are going to encrypt one of three possible plaintexts: 0, 1, or 2. As in the Caesar cypher, we are going to pick a key that is also either 0, 1, or 2 and add it to the plaintext. However, in this system, we will do the addition (mod 4). Thus, $f(plain, key) = plain + key$ (mod 4).

(a) Make a two-input function table for this encryption function.

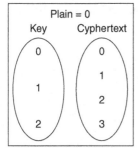

(b) Using the same method as above, describe the function as a collection of one-input functions where the plaintext is fixed for each function.

Plain = 0		Plain = 1		Plain = 2	
Key	Cyphertext	Key	Cyphertext	Key	Cyphertext
0	0	0	0	0	0
	1		1		1
1	2	1	2	1	2
2	3	2	3	2	3

(c) Now imagine you are Eve, and you observe a cyphertext of 3. How does this limit the possible plaintexts that could have been encrypted?

5

Probability Theory

5.1. Outcomes of an experiment

Consider an experiment that depends on chance, and that does not depend on any unknown information. What can we say about the outcome? If we actually carry the experiment out, we can say precisely what happened – but what can we say beforehand? The best description we can hope to give is one that specifies the likelihood of each possible outcome. Such a description is called a *probability distribution*. Probability theory is a way of reasoning about likelihoods.

Consider the roll of a die – there are six possible outcomes (not including wacky things like "the die rolls right off the table"). We implicitly assume that outcomes of a single experiment are *mutually exclusive*. That is, only one of the outcomes can occur each time that the experiment is performed.

The possible outcomes are shown in Figure 5.1.

The set of possible outcomes is called the *sample space*. It is also called the *probability space*.

5.2. Probabilities of outcomes

We describe the relative likelihoods of the six possible outcomes by assigning each outcome a number that represents its *probability*. If, for example, one outcome is twice as likely to occur as another, we assign the first outcome a probability twice that assigned to the second.

Certain conventions govern the numbers we use as probabilities. It would not make sense for one outcome to be -1 times as likely as another, so we restrict probabilities to be nonnegative numbers. We want probability 0 to correspond to impossibility; an outcome that never occurs would be assigned probability 0. We want probability 1 to correspond to certainty; an outcome

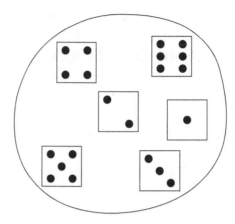

Figure 5.1. Probability space for rolling a single die.

that always occurs would be assigned probability 1. In a typical experiment, each outcome's probability is a number bigger than 0 and smaller than 1.

Here is a way to interpret probabilities for the outcome of our experiment. If you carried out exactly the same experiment thousands of times, the probability of some possible outcome is our best estimate as to the proportion of times that outcome occurs. For example, suppose we roll a die a thousand times. Our best estimate of the number of times we roll a 2 is 1/6 of 1000. The probability of rolling a 2 in the experiment is 1/6. We can write this as

$$\text{Prob}[\boxed{\cdot\ \cdot}] = 1/6$$

Similarly for the other outcomes:

$$\text{Prob}[\boxed{\cdot}] = 1/6, \ \text{Prob}[\boxed{\cdot\cdot}] = 1/6, \ \text{Prob}[\boxed{\cdot\ \cdot}] = 1/6$$
$$\text{Prob}[\boxed{\cdot\cdot\cdot}] = 1/6, \ \text{Prob}[\boxed{\cdot\cdot\ \cdot\cdot}] = 1/6$$

Formally, the probabilities of the outcomes are represented by a function (inevitably named p) whose domain is the sample space and whose codomain is the set of all numbers between 0 and 1.

5.3. Plotting a probability distribution

It is often useful to summarize the probabilities of the different outcomes using a bar graph. Along the horizontal axis we list the possible outcomes. The

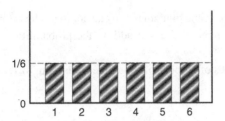

Figure 5.2. Probability distribution for rolling a single die.

vertical axis measures probability. The probability distribution for the number of pips on a single die is shown in Figure 5.2.

5.4. Probabilities of sets of outcomes

What is the probability of getting an even number? According to probability theory, in order to find the probability that one of several outcomes occurs, you can add up the probabilities of those outcomes. Thus the probability of getting ⚁, ⚃, or ⚅ is $1/6 + 1/6 + 1/6$.

We can similarly deduce that the probability of getting ⚀, ⚁, ⚂, ⚃, ⚄, or ⚅ is

$$\frac{1}{6} + \frac{1}{6} + \frac{1}{6} + \frac{1}{6} + \frac{1}{6} + \frac{1}{6}$$

which is 1. This is to be expected because it is certain that one of the six faces will occur (there are no other possible outcomes). In general, if you add up the probabilities of all possible outcomes of an experiment, you had better get 1.

5.5. Summary so far

- The possible outcomes of an experiment are *mutually exclusive*. (You can't have two of them happening at the same time.)
- The list of possible outcomes must be *exhaustive*. *One* of them must occur when you do the experiment.[1]
- Each possible outcome has a *probability*, a number between 0 and 1.

---

[1] Sometimes this is a mathematical idealization of the actual experiment. In a coin-flip experiment, it is in reality possible that the die rolls right off the table (or the coin lands on its edge, whatever), but we typically don't include such possibilities as outcomes in our probability space.

- For any set of possible outcomes, we can compute the probability that what occurs is a member of this set: add up the probabilities of the individual outcomes.
- The probabilities of all possible outcomes must sum to 1.

5.6. Uniform distributions

We can use the last fact to decide on probabilities for certain experiments. Suppose there are k outcomes, all equally likely (as in the case of rolling a die, where k is 6). What probabilities should we assign? We must assign the same probability to each outcome; let's use the variable x to stand for this unknown probability. Because the probabilities of all these outcomes must sum to 1, we have

$$\overbrace{x + x + \cdots + x}^{k \text{ terms}} = 1$$

That is, $kx = 1$. Solving for x, we get $x = 1/k$. Thus each outcome has probability $1/k$.

A probability distribution in which all the probabilities are the same is called a *uniform probability distribution* (often just *uniform distribution*). Let's consider another experiment: rolling two dice.

There are 36 possible outcomes (Figure 5.3), all equally likely. Hence each possible outcome has probability 1/36. This is another example of a uniform probability distribution.

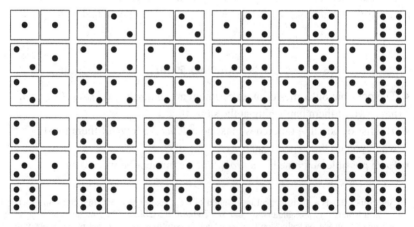

Figure 5.3. The 36 possible outcomes of the roll of two dice.

5.7. Random variables

Often we want to consider some quantity derivable from the outcome of an experiment. For example, in the case of rolling two dice, we are often interested in the total number of pips showing. We use the notion of a *random variable*. You can think of a random variable as a variable, say X, whose value depends on the outcome of an experiment. In the case of two dice, for example, one might say, "let X be the number of pips showing after a roll of two dice. What is the probability that X is 5?" We can compute this probability by going back to the possible outcomes of the experiment, as follows. (Note that we use "Prob[$X = 5$]" as mathese for "the probability that X is 5.")

$$\text{Prob}[X = 5] = \text{Prob}[\; \square\!\square \text{ or } \square\!\square \text{ or } \square\!\square \text{ or } \square\!\square \text{ or } \square\!\square \;]$$
$$= \text{Prob}[\square\!\square] + \text{Prob}[\square\!\square] + \text{Prob}[\square\!\square]$$
$$+ \text{Prob}[\square\!\square]$$
$$= \tfrac{1}{36} + \tfrac{1}{36} + \tfrac{1}{36} + \tfrac{1}{36}$$
$$= \tfrac{4}{36}$$

Here is another calculation. What is the probability that X is at least 10?

$$\text{Prob}[X \geq 10] = \text{Prob}[X = 10 \text{ or } X = 11 \text{ or } X = 12]$$
$$= \text{Prob}[X = 10] + \text{Prob}[X = 11] + \text{Prob}[X = 12]$$
$$= \text{Prob}[\square\!\square \text{ or } \square\!\square \text{ or } \square\!\square] + \text{Prob}[\square\!\square]$$
$$\text{or } \square\!\square] + \text{Prob}[\square\!\square]$$
$$= \tfrac{3}{36} + \tfrac{2}{36} + \tfrac{1}{36}$$
$$= \tfrac{6}{36}$$

The probability distribution for X is shown in Figure 5.4.

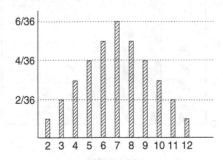

Figure 5.4. The probability distribution for X.

5.7.1. *Defining a random variable in terms of another random variable*

One can define new random variables in terms of previously defined random variables. Let $Y = (X - 7)^2$. Here is a table of values for X and Y.

X	Y
2	25
3	16
4	9
5	4
6	1
7	0
8	1
9	4
10	9
11	16
12	25

Note that there are, for example, two values of X, 2 and 12, for which Y is 25. The probability that Y is 25 is therefore the probability that X is 2 or 12. Because $\text{Prob}[X = 2]$ is 1/36, and $\text{Prob}[X = 12]$ is also 1/36, we can infer that $\text{Prob}[Y = 25]$ 1/36 + 1/36.

The probability distribution for Y is shown in Figure 5.5.

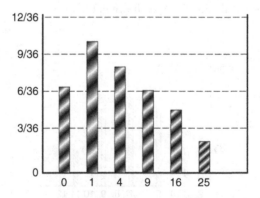

Figure 5.5. The probability distribution for Y.

5.7.2. Formal mathematical definition of random variables

Formally, a random variable is neither random nor a variable. (Discuss among yourselves.) It is a function whose domain is the sample space.

Thus the random variable X (number of pips showing after a roll of two dice) is really the function depicted in Figure 5.6.[2]

Reasoning about functions can thus be used to reason about random variables and vice versa. We use this sort of reasoning in connection with encryption functions.

5.7.3. Uniform distributions for random variables

Let's go back to the experiment where we roll a single die. Let Z be the modulo-3 representative for the number of pips showing after the roll. Then Z is a random variable, and Prob$[Z = 0] = 1/3$, Prob$[Z = 1] = 1/3$, and Prob$[Z = 2] = 1/3$. Is the probability distribution of Z a uniform distribution? Well, that depends. You can depict it in different ways (Figure 5.7).

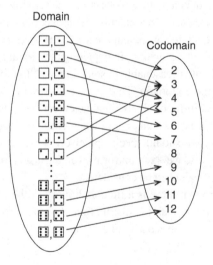

Figure 5.6. The random variable X, the number of pips showing after a roll of two dice, as a function.

---

[2] I don't really care what codomain this function has; in the diagram I just show the range, that is, the set of elements of the codomain that are images under the function. However, in Subsection 5.7.3 we see a reason why the codomain does sometimes matter.

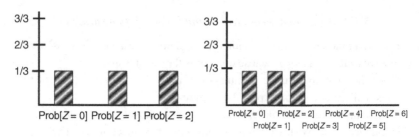

Figure 5.7. Different ways of depicting the probability distribution of the random variable Z.

It should be clear that whether a random variable is considered uniformly distributed depends on the values for which we plot the probability. That is, one can always throw in some values that have probability 0 (the random variable never takes on that value), and declare that the distribution is therefore not uniform (because there are other values having nonzero probability). Thus you need to be a little careful in deciding whether a random variable is uniformly distributed. We'll deal with this in two ways.

First, remember that a "random variable" is actually a function whose domain is the sample space. As a function, it has a codomain. (Recall also that the codomain may contain values that are not in the range; such values would have probability zero of occurring.) In depicting the probability distribution of the random variable, it is reasonable in some contexts to plot the probabilities of all elements of the codomain. Thus we would say the random variable is uniform if the probabilities of all codomain elements were the same.

A safer solution: when we talk about whether the distribution of a random variable is uniform, we should specify precisely what set of values is to be considered. To do this, we say "uniform over S" instead of just "uniform," where S is the set of values to be considered.

Mostly, be aware that there is a little ambiguity in the way the term "uniform" is applied to the probability distribution of a random variable. This issue arises when we analyze the security of a cryptosystem.

5.8. Problems

1. For each of the following figures, decide whether or not the figure shows a valid probability distribution, and if so, identify it as a uniform or non-uniform distribution.

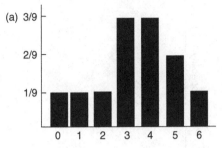

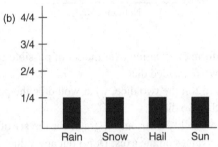

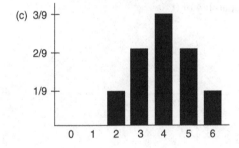

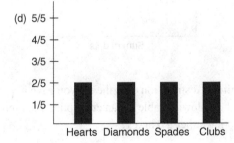

2. Consider a five-sided die.
   (a) The set of possible values for the die roll is the integers from 1 to 5. Draw the probability distribution graph for the set of these possible values, and label the values on the axes.

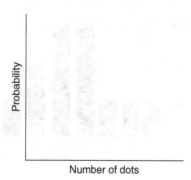

(b) Is this a uniform distribution over the set of possible values?

3. Now consider two five-sided dice.

    (a) If you were to roll the two dice, what would be the possible values for the sum of the two dice?

    (b) Draw the probability distribution graph for the set of possible values, and label the values on the axes. Don't put any values on the graph that have a probability of 0.

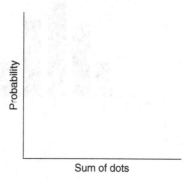

    (c) Is this a uniform distribution over the set you gave in part (a)?

4. Now consider the following table for an encryption function designed to be used for encrypting either a 0 or a 1.

		key			
		0	1	2	3
plain	0	1	1	1	0
	1	0	0	0	1

The corresponding one-input function obtained by specializing the the plaintext are as follows:

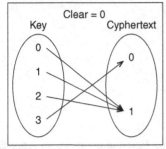 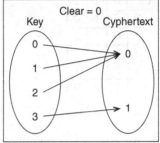

(a) Imagine an experiment in which the key is chosen uniformly at random. Let A be the random variable that is the encryption of plaintext 0. Draw the probability distribution of A.

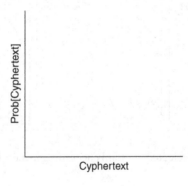

(b) Let B be the random variable that is the encryption of plaintext 1. Draw the probability distribution of B.

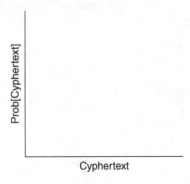

5. Consider the following table for a decryption function:

		key		
		0	1	2
	0	2	1	0
	1	0	1	2
	2	1	0	2
plain	3	2	0	1
	4	1	2	0
	5	0	2	1

(a) Fill in the arrows in the following function diagrams to represent the specializations of the above decryption function:

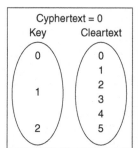

(b) Let the key be selected randomly according to a uniform distribution on {0,1,2}.

   i. Let A be the decryption of the cyphertext 0 using the random key. Draw the probability distribution of A.

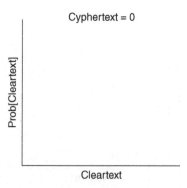

ii. Let *B* be the decryption of the cyphertext 1. Draw the probability distribution of *B*.

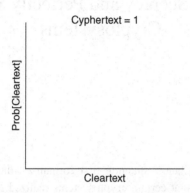

iii. Let *C* be the decryption of the cyphertext 2. Draw the probability distribution of *C*.

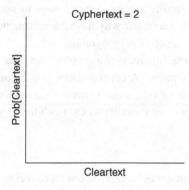

6

Perfect Secrecy and Perfectly Secure Cryptosystems

The mathematician Claude Shannon first formalized the notion of perfect secrecy and showed that certain cryptosystems realized it. We do not cover all of his theory, but address the part that is directly relevant to our study of cryptography and that relies on math that is within the scope of the text.

In this chapter, we discuss how to tell whether a cryptosystem is perfectly secure. In Chapter 7, we discuss some more ways to use perfect secrecy. It should become clear to the reader why modular arithmetic is used instead of ordinary arithmetic for much of cryptography.

As we will see, perfect secrecy of a cryptosystem and unique decryptability are mathematical cousins. A cryptosystem may be uniquely decryptable and *not* perfectly secure, or vice versa. However, the math that goes into determining perfect secrecy is very similar to the math that goes into determining unique decryptability.

6.1. What does an eavesdropper learn from seeing a cyphertext?

A cryptosystem is perfectly secure if an eavesdropper learns nothing about the plaintext from seeing the cyphertext. To understand what cryptosystems are secure, therefore, we consider what it means to learn something.

For this purpose, we consider a very simple scenario. Alice sends Bob an encrypted message, and Eve intercepts the cyphertext. (For now, we ignore the possibility that Bob may respond using the same cryptosystem and even the same key.) To understand what Eve has learned from seeing the cyphertext, we consider her knowledge of the plaintext before (her *a priori* knowledge) and after she sees the cyphertext (her *a posteriori* knowledge). We want to consider a very general model of what Eve knows because we don't want the security of our cryptosystem to depend on what kind of knowledge Eve possesses. We assume that Eve has a list (perhaps implicitly) of all the possible plaintexts Alice might have sent. Moreover, for each possible plaintext, Eve has assigned a positive number indicating how likely that possible plaintext is the true plaintext. That is, Eve has in mind a *probability distribution* for the true plaintext.

Now of course in reality the choice of plaintext is often not random at all. Typically Alice has a very specific message she wants to convey to Bob. However, right now we're studying this scenario from Eve's perspective, and to her the cleartext is as unpredictable as if it were chosen randomly. Thus as far as the mathematics is concerned, Eve reasons as if Alice chooses the plaintext randomly according to a particular probability distribution.

In principle, Eve's *a priori* knowledge of the plaintext might be represented by any probability distribution. However, for the sake of simplicity one would usually assume the distribution is uniform among some subset.

Example 1: Before seeing the cyphertext, Eve knows that the plaintext is a U.S. phone number, hence consists of ten digits. In this case, her *a priori* knowledge might assign the same probability to every 10-digit number.

If Eve is a little savvier still, she might have a more specific model of the plaintext. For example, she might consider possible only those 10-digit numbers whose first 3 digits form a valid area code. In this case, her probability distribution might be the uniform distribution over this set of numbers: all such numbers are assigned the same probability, and all other numbers are assigned probability 0.

Example 2: In a slight variant of an historical example, Eve might know in advance that the plaintext is either a 0 or a 1 (0 indicating that the British plan to attack by land, 1 indicating a sea attack). Based on her knowledge of British military tactics, Eve might consider a land attack more likely. In this case, she might assign probability 2/3 to a land attack and 1/3 to a sea attack.

What about Eve's *a posteriori* knowledge of the plaintext? That is, what does she know after having seen the cyphertext? Remember that we assume Eve knows the cryptosystem used by Alice and Bob (though she doesn't know the key). Eve knows that there is some key that decrypts the cyphertext to yield the plaintext. This sometimes provides some additional information about the plaintext.

Example 1a: Suppose the cryptosystem being used is the addition cypher where the block size is five digits. In this case the modulus is 10^5 and the key is a five-digit number. Let's say the two blocks of intercepted cyphertext are 37491...92722. Eve knows that for every U.S. area code the second digit is 0 or 1 (well, this *used* to be true). By examining the second digit of the first block of cyphertext, she can infer that the second digit of the key is 5, 6, or 7. By then examining the second digit of the second block of cyphertext, she can infer that the second digit of the second block of plaintext is 4, 5, 6, or 7. She didn't know this before seeing the cyphertext; thus she has learned at least a tiny bit about the plaintext from seeing the cyphertext.

Now we consider an arbitrary cryptosystem. Let $g(cyphertext, key)$ be the decryption function, and suppose b is the largest key allowed by the system (i.e., the key could be any number from 0 to b). Suppose Eve learns the cyphertext, and let c denote that cyphertext. Then she can infer that the plaintext is one of the following:

$$g(c, 0), g(c, 1), g(c, 2), \ldots, g(c, b)$$

She can combine this information with her *a priori* knowledge of the cyphertext to further narrow down the set of possibilities.

Example 3: Suppose the number of possible keys is 10^{30}. In this example, we won't specify the cryptosystem. Suppose Eve knows that the plaintext is an English sentence of length 75. There are roughly 2^{75} such sentences. Her *a priori* knowledge about the plaintext is represented by a probability distribution that is uniform over all such sentences.

Now she learns that the cyphertext is 7856...03457 (some particular 150-digit number). How many hypotheses for the plaintext are consistent with her two sources of knowledge, her *a priori* knowledge and her knowledge of the cyphertext? The answer depends on the cryptosystem and the particular cyphertext, but a good guess is that very few will be consistent—that only 1 or 2 or 10 or so of the possible decryptions of the cyphertext will be English text. Imagine that Eve tries all possible keys, decrypts the cyphertext with each, and discards the results that are not English text. She ends up retaining only a few possibilities. Thus in this example she can learn a great deal about the plaintext from the cyphertext.

There is a complicated formula that specifies the probabilities defining Eve's *a posteriori* knowledge of the plaintext in terms of her *a priori* knowledge and the cyphertext she intercepted. The formula uses a law of probability called Bayes' Law that helps in the calculation of probabilities that incorporate knowledge. We won't go into this formula. The special case that is important to us is when Eve's *a priori* knowledge of the plaintext is represented by a uniform distribution over some set S. In this case, Eve's *a posteriori* knowledge of the plaintext after learning the cyphertext is a uniform distribution over the intersection of the set S with the set of all possible decryptions of the cyphertext (i.e., the set $g(c, 0), g(c, l), \ldots$ obtained by trying all possible keys).

6.2. Evaluation of cryptosystems

Having studied the issues from Eve's perspective, let us turn to the perspective of some imaginary organization that is considering recommending the adoption of some cryptosystem, an agency we shall denote by NSO (standing for "No Such Organization"). The NSO wants to ensure that, if the cryptosystem is used correctly, it will be perfectly secure in that an eavesdropper Eve will learn nothing from a cyphertext.

Let's say we are evaluating a cryptosystem where the possible keys are the integers between 0 and s, the set of possible plaintexts are the integers between 0 and t, and the encryption function is $f(clear, key)$.

The NSO mandates that the key be chosen randomly with a uniform distribution over all possible keys. Thus for purposes of analysis, the key is a random variable K. The cyphertext is obtained by encrypting the plaintext with the key. Thus it depends on both the plaintext and the key. For each possible cleartext i, we let X_i denote the corresponding cyphertext. That is, X_i is defined by the equation $X_i = f(i, K)$. Note that because the key K is a random variable, so is X_i.

Here is the security requirement of perfect secrecy:

> **Perfect secrecy:** The probability distributions of the random variables $X_0, X_1, X_2, \ldots, X_t$ are all the same.

Thus if someone tells you just the probability distribution of one of the variables X_i, you couldn't tell which one it was, that is, which plaintext was used in producing it. If instead of telling you the probability distribution, she just gave you a number selected according to that distribution, you would again have no idea which variable X_i was used.

But this is precisely what Eve receives: a particular value of one of the random variables X_i, randomly chosen according to that variable's probability distribution. Because all these distributions are the same, Eve can learn nothing about the particular plaintext i. Her *a posteriori* knowledge is the same as her *a priori* knowledge.

Example 2a: Consider the cryptosystem where the encryption function is $f(plain, key) = plain + key$ rem 2. The only possible plaintexts are 1 and 0, and the only possible keys are 1 and 0. The key is chosen randomly. With probability 1/2, the key is 1 and with probability 1/2 the key is 0 .

- Suppose the plaintext is 1. What is the probability distribution of the cyphertext? With probability 1/2 the key will be 1, so the cyphertext will be $1 + 1 \equiv 0$. With probability 1/2 the key will be 0, so the cyphertext will be $1 + 0 \equiv 1$. Thus the cyphertext has probability 1/2 of being 0 and probability 1/2 of being 1.

- Suppose the plaintext is 0. What is the probability distribution of the cyphertext in this case? With probability 1/2 the key will be 1 so the cyphertext will be $0 + 1 \equiv 1$. With probability 1/2 the key will be 0 so the cyphertex will be $0 + 0 \equiv 0$. Thus the cyphertext has probability 1/2 of being 1 and probability 1/2 of being 0.

We see that this cryptosystem achieves perfect secrecy: for a key chosen uniformly at random; the probability distribution of the cyphertext doesn't depend on the plaintext.

Example 4: Consider a cryptosystem based on non-modular arithmetic, one where the encryption function is $f(plain, key) = plain + key$. Let us say the plaintext and key must be modulo-26 representatives. As a result, the cyphertext can be any number from 0 to 50. We assume the key is selected randomly and uniformly among $\{0, 1, 2, \ldots, 25\}$

- Suppose the plaintext is 0. In this case, the cyphertext is uniformly distributed among $\{0, 1, \ldots, 25\}$. The probability is 0 that 26 or 27 or ...... or 50 occur as the cyphertext.

- Suppose the plaintext is 1. In this case, the cyphertex is uniformly distributed among $\{1, 2, \ldots 26\}$.

- Suppose the plaintext is 25. In this case, the cyphertext is uniformly distributed among $\{25, 26, \ldots, 50\}$.

Clearly the probability distribution of the cyphertext depends crucially on the particular plaintext. Thus this system does not achieve perfect secrecy. Indeed, it is very likely, for example, that an eavesdropper who knows *a priori* that the plaintext is either 0 or 25 will be able to determine which it is after seeing the cyphertext. There is only one cyphertext, 25, that could have come from both those plaintexts.

Even the NSO can't be expected to consider each plaintext i separately and calculate the probability distribution of the corresponding cyphertext random variable X_i. Instead, they use the mathematical properties of the encryption function to show that perfect secrecy is achieved.

They use the following lemmata. (A lemma is a mathematical result that is proved to help in proving something else.) The proofs of the lemmata may seem hard to understand but the ideas are simple.

Lemma 1: Suppose $g(x)$ is an invertible function. Let X be an element of the domain of g, chosen randomly according to the uniform distribution. (That is, X is a random variable.) Then the corresponding output $g(X)$ is random and distributed uniformly among the elements of the codomain.

Proof: Let c be any element of the codomain. By definition of the inverse g^{-1} of g, the random codomain element $g(X)$ is equal to c whenever the random domain element X is equal to $g^{-1}(c)$. The probability that $X = g^{-1}(c)$ is one divided by the size of the domain. Hence the probability that $g(X) = c$ is one divided by the size of the domain.

We've shown that for any element of the codomain, the probability that $g(X)$ equals that element is one divided by the size of the domain. Because all the codomain elements have the same probability, the distribution of $g(X)$ is uniform.

Example 5: Consider as an example the function $g(x) = x + 3$ rem 4 with domain $\{0, 1, 2, 3\}$. The codomain is also $\{0, 1, 2, 3\}$. Suppose X is an element of the domain selected uniformly at random. That means that X has probability 1/4 of being 0, probability 1/4 of being 1, probability 1/4 of being 2, and probability 1/4 of being 3. Let $Y = f(X)$. Then Y is also a random variable. What is the probability that $Y = 0$? Well, $Y = 0$ would mean that $X = 1$, and this will happen with probability 1/4. What is the probability that $Y = 1$? Well, $Y = 1$ would mean that $X = 2$, and this will happen with probability 1/4. Similarly, the probability that $Y = 2$ is 1/4, and the probability that $Y = 3$ is 1/4. Thus Y is uniformly distributed among $\{0, 1, 2, 3\}$.

Lemma 2: For each plaintext i, define the function $f_{\text{plain}=i}(key)$ to be the specialization

$$f_{\text{plain}=i}(key) = f(i, key)$$

If for every plaintext i the function f_i is invertible then the cryptosystem with encryption function f achieves perfect secrecy.

Proof: Suppose the key K is chosen randomly according to the uniform distribution. Let i be any cleartext. The cyphertext is the random variable $f_i(K)$. By Lemma 1, the probability distribution of this random variable is uniform.

We have shown that no matter what plaintext i we start with, the probability distribution of the cyphertext is uniform. Thus the probability distribution of the cyphertext doesn't depend on which plaintext we start with. This shows that the cryptosystem achieves perfect secrecy.

Example 5a: Consider the mod 4 addition cypher. The encryption function is $f(plain, key) = plain + key$ rem 4. Suppose the key is chosen randomly according to the uniform distribution on $\{0, 1, 2, 3\}$.

- Suppose the plaintext i is 0. By plugging in 0 for the plaintext, we get the function

$$f_0(key) = 0 + key \text{ rem } 4$$

This is certainly an invertible function (in fact, the inverse of this function is itself). Hence, by Lemma 1, for a uniformly random key, the cyphertext is random uniform among $\{0, 1, 2, 3\}$.
- Suppose the plaintext i is 1. By plugging in 0 for the plaintext, we get the function

$$f_1(key) = 1 + key \text{ rem } 4$$

Because this is an invertible function, the cyphertext is random uniform among $\{0, 1, 2, 3\}$.
- You can try plaintext = 2 and plaintext = 3. In these cases as well the cyphertext is random uniform among $\{0, 1, 2, 3\}$.

No matter what the plaintext, the probability distribution of the corresponding cyphertext is uniform among $\{0, 1, 2, 3\}$. Thus the cryptosystem achieves perfect secrecy.

Example 1b: We again consider the addition cypher where the block size is five digits, the modulus is 10^5, and the key is a five-digit number. However, this time we will consider encrypting only one block instead of two. (If you want to securely encrypt a second block, you have to use another key.) The encryption function is

$$f(plain, key) = plain + key \text{ rem } 10^5$$

Let i be any plaintext (that is, any five-digit number). The function f_i defined earlier then has the rule

$$f_i(key) = i + key \text{ rem } 10^5$$

Thus this function modularly adds i to its input. Does this function have an inverse? Yes: the inverse of modularly adding i is modularly subtracting i. Thus the inverse is the function g_i defined by the rule

$$g_i(key) = key - i \text{ rem } 10^5$$

Hence by Lemma 2 the cryptosystem achieves perfect secrecy.

Example 1c: Now suppose we consider using the same cryptosystem but encrypt two blocks of plaintext using the same key. For example, say the plaintext is 40186 37600. The cyphertext also consists of two blocks. The first block of cyphertext is obtained by adding the key to 40186 (and taking the remainder). The second block of cyphertext is obtained by adding the key to 37600 (and taking the remainder). We can write the rule for this function as

$$h(key) = [40186 + i \text{ rem } 10^5, 37600 + i \text{ rem } 10^5]$$

Is this function invertible? No, it's not. For example, the cyphertext [40186, 40186] is not the image of any key under the function h. Thus the inverse cannot map 40186 40186 to anything. Thus the inverse is not a function.

> In fact, as we saw in Example 1a, this cryptosystem does not achieve
> perfect secrecy: Eve can learn about the plaintext from seeing the cypher-
> text. A way to see this in terms of probability distributions is as follows. If
> the plaintext is, say, 40186 37600 then with probability $1/10^5$ the key will
> be 59814 so the cyphertext will be 00000 97414. However, if the plaintext
> is instead 40186 37644 then the there is no key that produces the cypher-
> text 00000 97414 so the probability of that cyphertext occuring is 0. If Eve
> happens to see that cyphertext, therefore, she knows that plaintext is not
> 40186 37644.

6.3. Perfect secrecy versus unique decryptability

Let $f(plain, key)$ be the encryption function for a cryptosystem. We have
seen that the system achieves perfect secrecy if for every plaintext i, the
specialization $f_{plain=i}$ is an invertible function.

Recall that a cryptosystem achieves unique decryptability if for every key,
every element of f's domain is the encryption of precisely one plaintext. Another way of saying the same thing is that for every key k, the specialization
$f_{key=k}$ is an invertible function.

We see that determining whether a cryptosystem achieves unique decryptability is very similar to determining whether the cryptosystem achieves perfect
secrecy. The only difference is whether one considers the functions obtained
by plugging in keys or those obtained by plugging in plaintexts.[1] In view of this
similarity, we say an encryption function is *uniquely de-keyable* if, for every i,
the specialization $f_{plain=i}$ is invertible.

6.4. A brief history of perfect secrecy

6.4.1. Vernam's machine

In 1917, Gilbert Vernam, a 27-year-old who worked for AT&T, developed a
machine for encryption and decryption of telegraph messages. Joseph Mauborgne, a major in the army and head of the Signal Corps research and engineering
division, saw how to make it an unbreakable system. About 30 years later
Claude Shannon developed the theory of perfect secrecy and used it to prove
that Vernam's cypher indeed achieved perfect secrecy. As we shall see, such
security comes at a price.

---

[1] Of course, there are perfectly secret cryptosystems for which the specializations are not
invertible. Design one!

The basis for Vernam's invention is modulo 2 addition. As we saw in Example 2 a, encryption by modulo 2 addition achieves perfect secrecy. Modulo 2 arithmetic works with 1's and 0's only (called *binary digits*, or *bits*), so it is perfectly suited to implementation in the binary world of digital electronics. Modulo 2 addition has an additional advantage in application to cryptography. Because the modulo-2 representative of -1 is 1, subtracting 1 modulo 2 is the same as adding 1 modulo 2. Of course subtracting 0 is the same as adding 0. It follows that the decryption function-subtracting the key modulo 2-is the same as the encryption function-adding the key modulo 2.

When the modulus is 2 there are only two possible plaintexts, 1 and 0. In order to encrypt a longer plaintext, one represents it as a string of 1's and 0's (called *binary digits*, or *bits*) and encrypts the bits one by one, using a new random key for each bit. Thus the number of bits of key needed is the number of bits of plaintext to encrypt.

Converting human-produced plaintext into binary and back would be a painful task if done by hand. By the time Vernam took up cryptography, a machine – the teletypewriter – already existed that automated these processes.

The "Morse" code of the teletypewriter was Baudot code, named after its inventor, J. M. E. Baudot. Each symbol is represented by a string of five bits. There are 32 such strings, so 32 symbols can be represented in this way. The teletypewriter was a machine that transformed keypresses into electrical pulses, representing the 1's and 0's, to be sent over a wire. The machine could also read a punched paper tape, a strip of paper in which a long sequence of 1's and 0's were represented by the presence or absence of punched holes.

Vernam proposed using the teletypewriter to *combine* the bits coming from the paper tape with the bits generated by keypresses. Each time a key was pressed, five bits are generated corresponding to the symbol pressed. At the same time, the tape is advanced five positions, and five bits are read from the tape. The first of the bits generated by the keypress is added (mod 2) to the first of the bits read from the tape, and the resulting bit is sent across the wire. Each of the remaining four bits of the keypress are similarly combined with the remaining four bits read from the tape. By using the tape to store a long enough sequence of key bits, one could automatically encrypt an entire message.

A similar machine at the other end with an identical tape handled decryption. Bits received over the wire were added mod 2 to the corresponding bits stored on the tape.

One important advantage of Vernam's machine was that it integrated the encryption process with the transmission process. In previous years, one would have to first encrypt a message and then separately transmit the cyphertext.

Vernam did away with the intermediate step, increasing efficiency and reducing the likelihood of error.

The key tapes were produced in matching pairs. To produce five bits of key, a symbol was chosen randomly (drawn from a hat) and the corresponding key was pressed; the corresponding five bits would be punched in the two tapes. Then another symbol was chosen, and so on. Making the key tapes was still a somewhat painstaking process.

Early on, the key tapes were formed into loops so as to provide an endless stream of bits of key. As long as the encryption machine's tape and the decryption machine's tape were identical and were started at the same place, they would remain forever synchronized.

However, a loop of key does not provide perfect secrecy because the key eventually repeats. Mauborgne realized that any regular repetition would lead to insecurity. More important, he realized that if the tape were not looped – if each random bit of key were used only once – the system would be perfectly secure. Even if an eavesdropper had prior knowledge of the first half of the plaintext, intercepting the cyphertext for the second half would not help her because the key used for the second half has no relation to that used for the first half.

Despite efforts by AT&T to market Vernam's machine, it was not a commercial success. Businesses preferred to stay with the methods they knew. Even the U.S. government declined to use the unbreakable cryptosystem until much later, when World War II was approaching.

6.4.2. The one-time pad

Around the same time that Vernam and Mauborgne were bringing forth unbreakable cryptography in the United States, the same idea was discovered in Germany. Three cryptologists in the German Foreign Office – Werner Kunze, Rudolf Schauffier, and Erich Langlotz – came upon the idea of a random, nonrepeating key. They used addition modulo 10 instead of modulo 2. Moreover, their system was not incorporated into a machine; they stayed with the method of employing clerks to manually carry out encryption and decryption. Unlike Vernam, they were in a position to bring their system into government use: around 1922 the German diplomatic corps began to use the system.

The keys were maintained not on paper tape but on pads of paper. Each pad consisted of 50 numbered sheets of legal-size paper. Each sheet displayed 48 five-digit numbers. The pads were manufactured in pairs, so there existed only two copies of each pad. One copy of each pad was kept in Berlin, and one was provided to an embassy. Clerks would use the pads one sheet at a time, and would destroy each sheet once it had been used, so that it would not be used again. The system become known as the one-time pad.

6.5. The drawback of perfectly secret cryptosystems

If the one-time pad is perfectly secure, why would a government use any other system? The characteristic that provides perfect security also makes the system unwieldy: it consumes huge quantities of key. The amount of communication traffic that required encryption, especially in times of war, was enormous, and manufacture of the key pads could not keep up.

Furthermore, suppose there are many geographically separated parties (say, the communications clerks for regiments) who all need to communicate with each other securely. If they were using a traditional cryptosystem, they could all be provided with a single key to use for all their communication. Suppose, instead, they were to use a one-time pad system. There are two possibilities. The first is that each party has a different pad to communicate with every other party. This approach greatly increases the amount of key that must be manufactured and kept track of. The second possibility is for all the parties to use copies of a single key pad. However, in this case they must constantly communicate with each other to make sure that no two parties independently use the same sheet of the pad. For example, say there are four parties, A, B, C, and D. A communicates with B and C communicates with D. A must coordinate with B so that A and B don't inadvertently use the same sheet of the pad. Such coordination is quite difficult, especially in times of war. (What do you do when one of the parties is unreachable?)

In 1930 the Soviet Union adopted the one-time pad system for their military, diplomatic, commercial, intelligence, and counterintelligence communication. During the early years of World War II, however, they ran short of key pads. As a result, they were forced to misuse the system: multiple messages were encrypted using the same key. This situation may have arisen because of the above multiparty scenario, or perhaps simply because of limits on the speed with which the key pads could be manufactured. In fact, this misuse needn't have meant a breach of security. Typically one message encrypted with the key was fairly low-grade diplomatic traffic, for example, while the other was top-secret material related to espionage. Perhaps some cypher clerk reasoned that such use was likely to escape the notice of the intelligence services of other countries. Whatever the reason, this temporary lapse in security resulted in the attempted cryptanalysis by the United States and Great Britain of many thousands of messages between the Soviet Union and its representatives. This secret project was codenamed VENONA. Only some 1% of the messages were compromised, and of these typically only a few words were revealed. However, it was enough to shed some light on a subject of some interest to the West, the infiltration by Soviet spies of Britain's MI5, its intelligence forces.

6.6. Problems

1. While you are at the racetrack, a jockey friend of yours slips you a piece of paper with the results of five trial races run yesterday with the four horses in today's race. Unfortunately, you have forgotten what the key you agreed on was (although you do remember that it was chosen uniformly at random). You know that the message was encrypted using the following function:

plain (Horse)

		0 (Lucky Charms)	1 (Greased Lightning)	2 (Eight Ball)	3 (Great Scott)
	0	0	1	2	3
	1	1	2	3	0
	2	2	3	0	1
key	3	3	0	1	2
	4	2	3	0	1
	5	2	3	0	1
	6	2	3	0	1
	7	2	3	0	1

   Consider the information you can get by decrypting his message, "33333."
   (a) Given this cyphertext, what are the possible combinations of winning horses?
   (b) Which horse do you bet on in today's race? Why?

2. Imagine you are Eve, and you wake up one morning and learn that a message was sent from Alice to Bob in which one digit was encrypted by adding (mod 10) a randomly selected key to the plaintext.
   (a) As far as you know at this point, what are the possible cleartexts?
   (b) Imagine that an hour later, you learn the cyphertext. Now what are the cleartexts consistent with what you know?
   (c) Now say you wake up the following day, and learn that Bob has sent a message to Alice in which TWO digits were encrypted by randomly choosing a key and adding it to each of the digits (mod 10). Based on what you know, what are the possible plaintexts?

(d) Once again, after pondering this for an hour, you observe the cypher-text itself. Now what are the plaintexts consistent with what you know?

For each of the encryption functions described in Problems 3 to 8 below, answer the following questions.

(i) Is the function uniquely decryptable for every key? If so, define the decryption function using a rule. If not, give a key and two plaintexts that map to the same cyphertext.

(ii) Is the function uniquely de-keyable for every plaintext? If so, show that for every plaintext the function mapping the key to the cyphertext is invertible (by giving the rule for the inverse). If not, give a plaintext and two keys that map to the same cyphertext.

(iii) If part ii showed that the encryption function was not uniquely de-keyable, is it nevertheless perfectly secure? If so, sketch a probability distribution for the cyphertext, assuming uniformly random selection of keys. Be sure to label the vertical axis to show what the probability values are. If not, provide two different plaintexts for which the distribution of cyphertexts are different.

Example:
- *Rule: encrypt(plain, key) = plain · key* rem 10
- *Plaintext space: integers 0 through 9*
- *Key space: integers 0 through 9*
- *Cyphertext space: integers 0 through 9*
  (i) *Yes, this function is uniquely decryptable for every key. The rule for the decryption function is decrypt(cyph, key) = cyph − key* rem 10.
  (ii) *Yes, this function is uniquely de-keyable for every plaintext. The rule for the inverse is key = cyph − plain* rem 10.
  (iii) *The function is uniquely de-keyable, as demonstrated in part ii.*

Example:
- *Rule: encrypt(plain, key) = plain ·* key rem 10
- *Plaintext space: integers 0 through 9*
- *Key space: integers 0 through 9*
- *Cyphertext space: integers 0 through 9*
  (i) *This function is not uniquely decryptable for every key. If the key is 5, for instance, the plaintexts 6 and 8 both encrypt to 0.*
  (ii) *The function is also not perfectly de-keyable. If the plaintext is 2, the keys 3 and 8 both yield a cyphertext of 6.*
  (iii) *The plaintexts 3 and 4 have different cyphertext distributions.*

Example:
- *Rule: encrypt(plain, key) = (plain · key^2) rem 7*
- *Plaintext space: 1, 2, 4*
- *Key space: 1, 2, 3, 4, 5, 6*
- *Cyphertext space: 1, 2, 4*
  - (i) *Yes, this function is uniquely decryptable for every key. The rule for the decryption function is decrypt(cyph, key) = ($\frac{cyph}{key^2}$) rem 7.*
  - (ii) *No, this function is not uniquely de-keyable. If the plaintext is 1, the keys 3 and 4 both yield cyphertexts of 2.*
  - (iii) *Despite the fact that this function is not uniquely de-keyable, it is perfectly secure. The probability distribution is uniform. Each possible cyphertext has a probability of 1/3.*

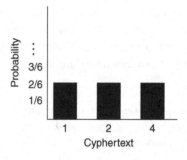

3. Rule: *encrypt(plain, key) = plain · key* rem 11
   Plaintext space: integers 1 through 10
   Key space: integers 1 through 10
   Cyphertext space: integers 1 through 10

4. Rule: *encrypt(plain, key) = plain^2 + key* rem 13
   Plaintext space: integers 0 through 12
   Key space: integers 0 through 12
   Cyphertext space: integers 0 through 12

5. Rule: *encrypt(plain, key) = plain + key^2* rem 7
   Plaintext space: integers 0 through 6
   Key space: integers 0 through 6
   Cyphertext space: integers 0 through 6

6. Rule: *encrypt(plain, key) = 4 · plain + key^2* rem 14
   Plaintext space: integers 0 through 13

Key space: integers 0 through 13
Cyphertext space: integers 0 through 13

7. Rule: $encrypt(plain, key) = (plain \cdot key^2)$ rem 5
   Plaintext space: 1,4
   Key space: 1,2, 3, 4
   Cyphertext space: 1, 4

8. Rule: $encrypt(plain, key) = plain + key$
   Plaintext space $= 0, 1, 2, 3$
   Key space $= 0, 1, 2, 3$
   Cyphertext space $= 0, 1, 2, 3, 4, 5, 6$

Below are tables for different encryption functions to be used to encrypt each block of a message. A key will be chosen uniformly at random for each block. For each encryption function, briefly answer the following two questions:

(a) Does it achieve perfect secrecy? If not, why not?
(b) Does it achieve unique decryptability? If not, why not?

9.

		Key			
		A	B	C	D
Plain	1	?	!	#	@
	2	!	#	@	?
	3	#	@	?	!
	4	@	?	!	#

10.

		Key			
		A	B	C	D
Plain	1	?	!	#	@
	2	!	?	@	?
	3	#	@	!	?
	4	@	#	?	!

11.

		Key			
		A	B	C	D
Plain	1	!	!	!	!
	2	?	?	?	?
	3	#	#	#	#
	4	@	@	@	@

12.

Key

Plain	A	B	C	D
1	!	?	#	@
2	?	#	@	!
3	#	@	!	?

13.

Key

Plain	A	B	C	D
1	#	@	!	?
2	@	!	?	#
3	!	?	#	@
4	?	#	@	!
5	!	@	?	#

14. Abbot and Costello work for the NSO, evaluating the security of crypto-systems. They receive the following table as a proposal for an encryption function.

Key

Plain	A	B	C	D
1	@	$	%	#
2	#	%	$	@
3	%	#	@	$
4	$	@	#	%

Abbot says

"This system has the following property: For each key, a plaintext chosen randomly according to the uniform distribution (over all possible plaintexts) encrypts to a cyphertext chosen randomly according to the uniform distribution (over all possible cyphertexts). Therefore the system achieves perfect secrecy."

Costello responds

"Abbott, you're wrong. The system does achieve perfect secrecy but not for the reason you give. In fact, I can rearrange the cyphertexts in the table so as to give an encryption function that has the property you cite but that does not achieve any kind of secrecy!"

Costello is correct.

(a) Show how to rearrange the cyphertexts in the table so as to get an encryption function that has the property Abbot cites but obviously does not achieve secrecy.

	Key			
	A	B	C	D
1				
Plain 2				
3				
4				

(b) Why does the originally proposed encryption achieve perfect secrecy? Explain by referring specifically to the table.

15. Consider the following encryption function:

$$\text{Plainspace: } 0, 1, 2, 3, 4$$

$$\text{Keyspace: } 0, 1, 2, 3, 4$$

$$\text{Cypherspace: } 0, 1, 2, 3, 4$$

$$f(plain, key) = plain^3 + key^2 \text{ rem } 5$$

(a) For each possible key k, the corresponding specializaiton of the encryption function, $Encrypt_{key=k}$, is a function whose domain is the set of plaintexts and whose codomain is the set of cyphertexts. Sketch each of these specialization functions below.

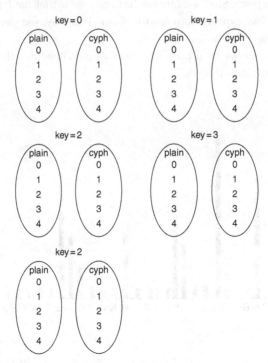

(b) Is the function uniquely decryptable?

(c) Is the encryption function uniquely de-keyable?

(d) Does the encryption method achieve perfect secrecy? If so, explain why; if not, suggest a function with the same keyspace, plainspace, and cypherspace that does.

16. Each night at 2:00 am, the *Boston Globe* sends its text for the next morning's paper over the phone lines to the printing presses. The text consists of 50,000 symbols, each represented by a number from 0 to 29. Thus the text is represented by a sequence of 50,000 numbers. For security, the Globe encrypts this sequence using a one-time pad. Each cyphertext number is the mod 30 sum of the corresponding plaintext and key numbers.

The *Providence Journal* has heard rumors that the *Boston Globe* will publish a story on the real reason the Patriots won't move to Rhode Island. The *Journal* wants to get the story so as to scoop the *Globe*. They hire Eve, renowned for her eavesdropping skills, to intercept the *Globe*'s cyphertext as it makes its way to the printing presses. Eve is to intercept the cyphertext and send it by modem to the *Journal's* Department of Sneaky Stunts.

Eve takes the job but has no desire to crawl down sewers and up telephone poles. She therefore hatches a scheme to trick the Journal by making up a fake cyphertext to send to them. That way, she can stay warm and comfortable at home.

She knows from previous issues of the Globe that the distribution of symbols is as follows.

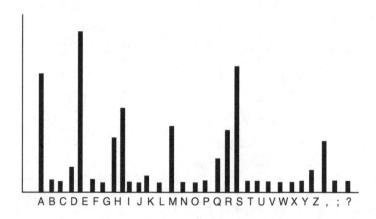

She comes up with the following distribution of numbers.

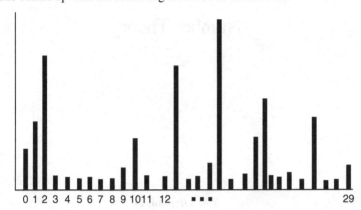

She generates a sequence of 50,000 numbers, each chosen according to the above distribution, and sends this sequence to the *Journal*.

(a) Why does the *Journal* realize she has tried to fool them? Explain precisely and specifically.

(b) How could Eve have successfully fooled the *Journal*? Explain precisely and specifically.

7

Number Theory

7.1. Divisibility

We say an integer b *evenly divides* another integer c if c/b is a whole number. Actually, nobody in mathematics ever says that b "evenly divides" c – people just say b "divides" c. Another way to say the same thing is to say that b is a *divisor* of c. The divisors of c are the numbers that (evenly) divide c. Finally, one can also say that b is *divisible* by c.

Examples:

- 3 divides 12.
- 3 is a divisor of 9.
- 40 is not a divisor of 20.
- 40 is divisible by 20.
- 4 divides 4.
- 5 is a divisor of -10.
- 12 divides 60.
- The positive divisors of 50 are 1, 2, 5, 10, 25, and 50.

7.2. Relative primality

Two numbers r and s are *relatively prime* if there is no integer bigger than 1 that is both a divisor of r and a divisor of s. We also say in this case that r is relatively prime to s. For example, 18 and 8 are *not* relatively prime because 2 is a divisor of both of them. On the other hand, 9 and 8 are relatively prime because the only divisors common to both of them are 1 and -1. We never count 1 and -1 as common divisors when determining relative primality.

- 20 and 40 are not relatively prime – for example, 20 is a common divisor.

- 27 and 80 are relatively prime. The only divisors of 27 that are bigger than 1 are 3, 9, and 27, all powers of 3, and 3 doesn't divide 80.
- 17 is relatively prime to 27.
- 17 and 0 are not relatively prime because 17 is a divisor of both.
- 1 and 6 are relatively prime because the only positive divisor of 1 is 1.

7.3. Prime numbers

A number n bigger than one is *prime* if its only positive divisors are 1 and itself. Thus the first few prime numbers are 2, 3, 5, 7, 11, 13, 17, 19, 23, 29, and 31. The only even prime number is 2 because any other even number has 2 as a divisor. We don't count 1 as a prime number.

Suppose n is a prime number. What numbers are relatively prime to n? Because n's only divisor bigger than 1 is n itself, any number not divisible by n is relatively prime to n. The nonnegative integers that *are* divisible by n are $0, n, 2n, 3n$, and so on.

7.4. Prime factorization

The factorization of 60 is the process of determining the primes whose product is 60. Clearly 6 is a divisor, and $6 \cdot 10 = 60$. But 6 and 10 are not primes, so we must factorize these numbers further. Now 6 is the product of the primes 2 and 3, and 10 is the product of the primes 2 and 5. We have

$$6 = 2 \cdot 3$$

$$10 = 2 \cdot 5$$

Multiplying these equations together, we get

$$6 \cdot 10 = 2 \cdot 3 \cdot 2 \cdot 5$$

Thus the prime factorization of 60 is 2, 2, 3, and 5. Note that 2 occurs twice in this list because it has to be multiplied in twice.

Let's try factorizing 60 in a different way. We observe that 60 is even, so 2 is a divisor. Dividing 60 by 2, we get 30. Now 30 is also even, so 2 is a divisor. Dividing by 2, we get 15. Finally, 15 is the product of 3 and 5. Thus the prime factorization is again 2, 2, 3, and 5.

A fundamental result in number theory is that the prime factorization of a positive number doesn't depend on how it is found, that there is one and only one prime factorization.

7.5. Euler's phi function $\phi(x)$

The mathematician Leonhard Euler defined the function $\phi(x)$ by the rule

$\phi(x)$ = the number of mod-x representatives that are relatively prime to x

In this book, we use two formulas for $\phi(x)$:

If m is a prime number then $\phi(m) = m - 1$.

This formula holds because every number from 0 to $m-1$ is relatively prime to m except 0.

If m is the product of two distinct primes p and q then $\phi(m) = (p-1) \cdot (q-1)$.

This formula holds because every number from 0 to $m-1$ is relatively prime to m except the following numbers.

$$0 \cdot p, 1 \cdot p, 2 \cdot p, \ldots, (q-1) \cdot p$$

and

$$0 \cdot q, 1 \cdot q, 2 \cdot q, \ldots, (p-1) \cdot q$$

There are $q - 1$ in the first list and $p - 1$ in the second list, for a total of $(q-1) + (p-1)$, except that 0 appeared in both list, so the real total is $(q-1) + (p-1) - 1$. Thus the number of numbers from 0 to $m - 1$ that are relatively prime is the total number of numbers from 0 to $m - 1$, namely m, minus the number that are not relatively prime, namely $(q-1) + (p-1) - 1$. Replacing m by pq, we get

$$\phi(pq) = pq - ((q-1) + (p-1) - 1)$$

Note that $(p-1) \cdot (q-1) = pq - q - p + 1$, which is the same as $pq - ((q-1) + (p-1) - 1)$. Thus $\phi(pq) = (p-1) \cdot (q-1)$.

When p and q are small numbers, $\phi(pq)$ is noticeably smaller than pq. For example, $\phi(6)$ is $(2-1) \cdot (3-1)$, which is 2. Another example: $\phi(15) = 8$.

However, when p and q get really big, pq is enormous, so the difference between pq and $pq - ((q-1) + (p-1) - 1)$ is really not so significant. For example, say $p = 9871$ and $q = 9533$. Then $pq = 94100243$ and $\phi(pq) = 94080840$. If you picked a random number between 0 and $pq - 1$, it would most likely be relatively prime to pq.

7.6. Exponentiation

Before discussing the uses of Euler's function, we briefly review exponentiation. We have used expressions such as 10^{20}, and readers will likely remember that this expression stands for

$$\underbrace{10 \cdot 10 \cdot 10 \cdot 10 \cdot 10 \cdot 10 \cdot 10 \cdot 10 \cdot 10 \cdot 10 \cdot 10 \cdot 10 \cdot 10 \cdot 10 \cdot 10 \cdot 10 \cdot 10 \cdot 10 \cdot 10 \cdot 10}_{20 \text{ times}}$$

The base (10, in this case) tells us what number to multiply times itself, and the exponent (20, in this case) tells us how many times to multiply the base by itself.

7.6.1. The rule for adding exponents

We can break up the multiplications thus:

$$\underbrace{10 \cdot 10 \cdot 10 \cdot 10 \cdot 10}_{\text{five times}} \cdot \underbrace{10 \cdot 10 \cdot 10 \cdot 10 \cdot 10 \cdot 10 \cdot 10 \cdot 10 \cdot 10 \cdot 10 \cdot 10 \cdot 10 \cdot 10 \cdot 10 \cdot 10}_{15 \text{ times}}$$

which shows that

$$10^5 \cdot 10^{15} = 10^{20}$$

This is an example of a general rule for exponentiation:

The rule for adding exponents: $b^{c+d} = b^c b^d$

In words, adding exponents corresponds to multiplying the exponential expressions.

7.6.2. The rule for multiplying exponents

We can also break up the multiplications into five groups of four:

$$\underbrace{10 \cdot 10 \cdot 10 \cdot 10}_{\text{four times}} \underbrace{10 \cdot 10 \cdot 10 \cdot 10}_{\text{four times}} \underbrace{10 \cdot 10 \cdot 10 \cdot 10}_{\text{four times}} \underbrace{10 \cdot 10 \cdot 10 \cdot 10}_{\text{four times}} \underbrace{10 \cdot 10 \cdot 10 \cdot 10}_{\text{four times}}$$

which we can rewrite as

$$10^4 \cdot 10^4 \cdot 10^4 \cdot 10^4 \cdot 10^4$$

Note that we are multiplying 10^4 by itself five times. This is the same as raising 10^4 to the power of five, that is, $(10^4)^5$. Thus we have shown that

$$10^{20} = (10^4)^5$$

This is an example of another general rule for exponentiation:

The rule for multiplying exponents: $b^{c \cdot d} = (b^c)^d$

In words, multiplying exponents corresponds to exponentiating by the first exponent, and then exponentiating the result by the second exponent.

7.7. Euler's Theorem

Now we give a theorem that is very important for a cryptographic scheme described in Chapter 14.

Euler's Theorem: For any modulus m, for any number b that is relatively prime to m,

$$b^{\phi(m)} \equiv 1 \pmod{m}$$

We can use this theorem to simplify exponential expressions. For example, let the modulus m be 4001, a prime. Then $\phi(m) = 4000$. Let b be a positive number less than 4001. Then

$$b^{8003} = b^{2 \cdot 4000 + 3} = (b^{4000})^2 b^3$$

where we have used the two rules of exponentiation outlined in Section 7.6.

Because $b^{4000} \equiv 1 \pmod{400}$, we can simplify mod 4001 expressions by replacing b^{4000} with 1.

$$(b^{4000})^2 b^3 \equiv (1)^2 b^3 \equiv b^3 \pmod{4000}$$

Similarly we can show

$$b^3 \equiv b^{12003} \equiv b^{16003} \equiv b^{20003} \pmod{4000}$$

and so on. The exact exponent doesn't matter; what matters is the mod-$\phi(m)$ representative of the exponent.

7.8. Problems

1. For each of the following pairs of numbers, say whether or not the two numbers are relatively prime.
   (a) 18, 4
   (b) 7, 27
   (c) 24, 33
   (d) 22, 51
   (e) 0, 17
2. For each of the following numbers n, list the nonnegative numbers less than n that are relatively prime to n, and use this list to find $\phi(n)$.
   (a) 18
   (b) 23

(c) 77

(d) 16

(e) 15

3. Use the rules of exponentiation to simplify each of the following formulae.

(a) $\frac{x^{15}}{x^7/(xy)^8}$

(b) $(x^{20})^{(y^5y^{10}-y^{15})}$

(c) $y^{15} - \frac{y^4y^6}{y^3y^8}$

In the following problems you will use Euler's Theorem and your knowledge of modular arithmetic to simplify a modular exponential expression b^t rem m to a similar expression where the exponent is a small nonnegative integer. You should assume that the base b is relatively prime to m so that Euler's Theorem is applicable. Show your work.

Example:

Question: modulus $m = 4001$ (a prime). Simplify b^{12006} rem m.

Answer: $\phi(m) = 4000$. We simplify as follows.

$$b^{12006} = b^{3\cdot4000+6} = (b^{4000})^3 b^6$$

Because $b^{4000} \equiv 1 \pmod{m}$ by Euler's Theorem, we can simplify $(b^{4000})^3 b^6$ rem m to $(1)^3 b^6$ rem m, which is b^6 rem m.

4. In this problem we use the modulus $m = 17$.

(a) Simplify b^{19} rem 17.

(b) Simplify b^{33} rem 17.

(c) Simplify b^{52} rem 17.

(d) Simplify b^{213} rem 17.

5. In this problem we use the modulus $m = 61$.

(a) Simplify b^{61} rem 61.

(b) Simplify b^{185} rem 61.

(c) Simplify b^{2410} rem 61.

6. In this problem we use the modulus $m = 143$.

(a) Simplify b^{225} rem 143.

(b) Simplify b^{481} rem 143.

(c) Simplify b^{12037} rem 143.

7. Which of the following equations are true? Which are false?

(a) Is $b^{21} \equiv b^4 \pmod{17}$?

(b) Is $b^{28} \equiv b^6 \pmod{23}$?

(c) Is $b^{59} \equiv b^{125} \pmod{67}$?

(d) Is $b^{540} \equiv b^{77}$ (mod 463)?

(e) Is $b^{723} \equiv b^5$ (mod 719)?

8. Solve for s or explain why no solution exists.

(a) $(b^5)^s \equiv b$ (mod 35)

(b) $(b^6)^s \equiv b$ (mod 23)

(c) $(b^{101})^s \equiv b$ (mod 7)

(d) $(b^7)^s \equiv b$ (mod 33)

8

Euclid's Algorithm

In Section 4.3.3 of Chapter 4, we introduced the notion of *modular multiplicative inverses*: for a modulus m, two integers a and b are mod-m multiplicative inverses if $a \cdot b \equiv 1 \pmod{m}$. In Section 4.3.4, we demonstrated a method for finding mod-m multiplicative inverses: write down the mod-m multiplication table for all mod-m representatives, and search for ones in the table. In Section 4.3.5, we observed that, for the modulus 6, some integers don't have multiplicative inverses, even integers that are not congruent mod-6 to 0. The method we present in this chapter will explain this phenomenon.

In this chapter, we describe a good algorithm for calculating modular multiplicative inverses. The algorithm is an extension of one attributed to the classical mathematician Euclid, who supposedly lived around 300 B.C. He is known primarily for his contribution to and systematization of geometry, but his famous book *Elements* also addressed number theory.

8.1. The measuring puzzle

Suppose you are given two containers and told how many cups of water each one can hold. You are also given an empty basin that can hold an unlimited amount of water. What is the smallest positive number of cups you can leave in the basin by using these two containers? The rules of the puzzle allow you to fill either container with water either from the tap or the basin, and to pour the water from the container either down the drain or into the basin.

For example, with a 7-cup container and a 5-cup container, you can leave a mere one cup of water in the basin. First, fill the seven-cup container from the tap and pour the water into the basin. Do this a total of three times. The basin now contains 21 cups of water. Next, fill the 5-cup container from the basin and pour the water down the drain. Do this a total of four times. You have removed 20 cups of water from the basin, leaving 1 cup.

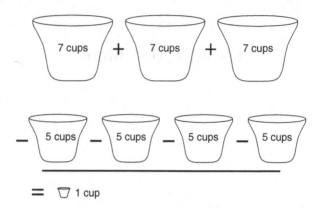

Figure 8.1. The solution to a puzzle with a 7-cup container and a 5-cup container.

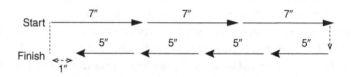

Figure 8.2. The same puzzle but with sticks instead of cups.

For those who prefer geometry, we can rephrase this puzzle in geometric terms. You are given two sticks and told each stick's length in inches. You want to measure off as small a (positive) distance as possible. Rephrasing the above example, if you are given a 7-inch stick and a 5-inch stick, you can measure off a 1-inch distance. As illustrated in Figure 8.2, you use the 7-inch stick to find the point p 21 inches to the right of the origin, and then use the 5-inch stick to find the point 20 inches to the left of p.

Note that one cup (or 1 inch) is the best answer one can hope for. We assume that every container can hold a whole number of cups (we say its capacity is an integer, that is, is *integral*) and we are using each container an integral number of times. Thus the number of cups of water in the basin remains integral throughout the process. The smallest positive integer, of course, is 1.

The solution to this puzzle is not just the final amount (1) but the way to achieve it (add 7 cups three times, then subtract 5 cups four times). The solution can be written compactly as a mathematical equation:

$$1 = 3 \cdot 7 - 4 \cdot 5$$

that tells us how many times to add 7 (three times) and how many times to add 5 (negative four times).

8.1.1. A more complicated example

Suppose you are given a container of capacity 524 and one of capacity 876. How small a number of cups can you leave in the basin? We earlier argued that throughout the process the number of cups in the basin remains integral. Let's use the same kind of argument to show that, for these container sizes, the number of cups in the basin remains a multiple of four.

Initially the basin contains zero cups of water, and zero is a multiple of four. Every time you pour water into the basin from the small container, you increase by 524 the number of cups of water in the basin. Note, however, that 524 is a multiple of 4, so you have added a multiple of 4 to a multiple of 4. Similarly, every time you fill the small container from the basin, you decrease by 524 the number of cups of water in the basin, thereby subtracting a multiple of 4 from a multiple of 4. The capacity of the large container, 876, is also a multiple of 4, so the same argument applies when you fill the basin from that container or fill that container from the basin. Thus no matter what you do, as long as you follow the rules, the number of cups of water in the basin will always be a multiple of 4.

The smallest positive multiple of 4 is 4 itself, so the best we can hope for is to leave a multiple of four cups in the basin. In fact, we can achieve precisely that: we fill the basin from the small container 107 times, and fill the large container from the basin 64 times, each time emptying the large container into the drain. (An astonishing waste of water, you might say, but precision has its price.) Mathematically, our accomplishment can be written as

$$4 = 107 \cdot 524 - 64 \cdot 876$$

8.2. Finding a modular multiplicative inverse by solving a measuring puzzle

What does the measuring puzzle have to do with modular multiplicative inverses?

Example 1

Suppose your modulus is 7, and you want to calculate a multiplicative inverse of 5. To solve this problem, take one container with a capacity of seven cups and one of capacity five. We saw above that we can use such containers to leave one cup of water in the basin; the method for doing so is expressed mathematically as the equation

$$1 = 3 \cdot 7 - 4 \cdot 5$$

Subtracting $-4 \cdot 5$ on both sides yields

$$1 - (-4 \cdot 5) = 3 \cdot 7$$

This equation shows that the difference between 1 and $-4 \cdot 5$ is a multiple of 7. That is,

$$-4 \cdot 5 \equiv 1 \quad (\text{mod } 7)$$

Thus -4 is a multiplicative inverse of 5. Success!

Example 2

Your modulus is 782394. You need to find a multiplicative inverse of 387451. Consider the measuring game using a container with capacity 782394 and another container with capacity 387451. It turns out that one can end up leaving one cup of water in the basin, and that the corresponding equation is

$$1 = -58490 \cdot 782394 + 118111 \cdot 387451$$

This equation shows that $118111 \cdot 387451$ is congruent to 1 (because it differs from 1 by a multiple of the modulus), and that therefore 118111 is a multiplicative inverse of 387451. Success again!

So far we have been fortunate. In the next example, not so much.

Example 3

The modulus is 876 and you want to find a multiplicative inverse of 524, that is, an integer q such that $1 - q \cdot 524$ is a multiple of 876. "A multiple of 876" means some integer times 876; let us use p to refer to that integer. For us to succeed, therefore, there must be integers p and q such that $1 - q \cdot 524 = p \cdot 876$. Are there any such integers?

Adding $q \cdot 524$ to both sides yields the equation

$$1 = p \cdot 876 + q \cdot 524 \tag{8.1}$$

The existence of integers p and q satisfying this equation would imply that there was a way to put exactly one cup of water in the basin using containers of size 524 and 876. We argued in Section 8.1.1 that this was impossible. Therefore 524 does not have a mod-876 multiplicative inverse!

The argument in Section 8.1.1, boiled down, is as follows. Assume that Eq. (8.1) is true for some integers p and q. Because 4 is a divisor of both 876 and 524, it is also a divisor of $p \cdot 876 + q \cdot 524$ for any integers p and q. If Eq. (8.1) were true then it would follow that four is a divisor of one, so the equation cannot be true.

8.3. Euclid's algorithm

In this section, we outline Euclid's algorithm and how it helps us.

8.3.1. What Euclid's algorithm computes

For any input integers a and b, Euclid's algorithm computes three integers s, t, and d, with three properties:

$$d > 0 \tag{8.2}$$
$$d = s \cdot a + t \cdot b \tag{8.3}$$
$$d \text{ is a divisor of } a \text{ and a divisor of } b. \tag{8.4}$$

These properties seem innocent but together they are quite powerful. They allow us to draw two conclusions. We now state these conclusions and provide the mathematical proofs. Try to follow the proofs but don't worry if they don't click for you.

Conclusion 1: d is the *largest* integer that divides both a and b.
Proof: Any other integer e that is a divisor of both a and b is therefore also a divisor of both $s \cdot a$ and $t \cdot b$, and is therefore a divisor of $s \cdot a + t \cdot b$, which is equal to d. Because e is a divisor of d and d is positive, we conclude that e is smaller than d.

Conclusion 2: d is the *smallest* positive number of cups of water that can be put in the basin using containers of capacity a and b.
Proof: Consider any pouring plan using containers of capacity a and b. Suppose water is poured p times from the container of capacity a and water is poured q times from the container of capacity b. (The numbers p

and q can be positive or negative.) The amount of water left in the basin is $p \cdot a + q \cdot b$.

Because d is a divisor of a, it is also a divisor of $p \cdot a$. Because d is a divisor of b, it is also a divisor of $q \cdot b$. Because d is a divisor of $p \cdot a$ and of $q \cdot b$, it is also a divisor of their sum, $p \cdot a + q \cdot b$. This shows that d is a divisor of the number of cups of water left in the basin by the pouring plan. Therefore d is smaller than or equal to the number of cups left in the basin by the plan.

Because of Conclusion 1, d is called the *greatest common divisor* of a and b. Euclid's algorithm is said to be an algorithm for finding the greatest common divisor. However, we are also interested in the integers s and t found by Euclid's algorithm:

- If the greatest common divisor is 1 then Eq. (8.3) shows that t is a mod-a multiplicative inverse of b.
- If the greatest common divisor is greater than 1 then Conclusion 2 implies that there are no integers p and q for which $1 = p \cdot a + q \cdot b$, and therefore b does not have a mod-a multiplicative inverse.

In Chapter 7, we introduced a term for integers a and b whose greatest common divisor is 1: we say that they are relatively prime. Euclid's algorithm therefore teaches us that a mod-a multiplicative inverse of b exists precisely when a and b are relatively prime.

8.3.2. The **forward** *direction*

We illustrate Euclid's algorithm with an example. Let's say we have a 12-cup container and a 5-cup container. We can make the big container act like a container of capacity 2, that is, we can use it to add 2 cups to the basin or subtract two cups from the basin. Suppose we want to add 2 cups.

- We fill the big container with water from the tap.
- We fill the small container with water from the big container, and pour the small container's water down the drain.
- We do the previous step again.
- Now the big container contains two cups of water. We pour the water into the basin.

A similar procedure can be used to remove 2 cups of water from the basin. Thus for the purpose of solving the puzzle, we can imagine that we have an (artificial) 2-cup container and a 5-cup container. Let's try to solve this new puzzle.

Now we show that we can make the 5-cup container act like a 1-cup container. Suppose we want to add one cup.

- We fill the 5-cup container with water from the tap.
- We fill the 2-cup container with water from the 5-cup container, and pour it down the drain.
- We do it again.
- Now the 5-cup container has one cup of water in it.

Of course, now that we know how to make the 5-cup container act like a 1-cup container, we can solve the puzzle directly by simply filling the 1-cup container and pouring the one cup of water into the basin.

Let's try another example.

- Suppose we start with a 44-cup container and a 13-cup container. We imagine the big container is a 5-cup container. (We fill the big container, and remove 13 cups from it three times, leaving 5 cups in it.)
- Now we need to solve a puzzle with a 13-cup container and an (artificial) 5-cup container. We can pretend the 13-cup container is a 3-cup container. (We fill the 13-cup container, and remove five cups from it twice.)
- Now we need to solve a puzzle with a 5-cup container and a 3-cup container. We can pretend the 5-cup container is a 2-cup container. (Fill the 5-cup container, and remove 3 cups from it.)
- We need to solve a puzzle with a 3-cup container and a 2-cup container. We can pretend the 3-cup container is a 1-cup container. (We fill the 3-cup container, and then remove two cups from it.)
- We need to solve a puzzle with a 2-cup container and a I-cup container. Solving the puzzle when you have a 1-cup container is easy!

The rule for creating artificial containers is as follows. If you have an x-cup container and a y-cup container and $x > y$, imagine that instead you have a y-cup container and an x rem y container. (Recall that x rem y is the remainder when x is divided by y.) Next, apply the same rule to the new containers, replacing the y-cup container with an artificial container, and so on, until the remainder (which would be the capacity of a new, smaller cup) turns out to be zero. The capacity of the corresponding larger cup is the smallest positive amount we can leave in the basin.

We go through one more example, but this time we do it in mathese rather than in terms of cups.

1. We start with 77 and 23. When 77 is divided by 23, the remainder is 8. Our new capacities are 23 and 8.
2. When 23 is divided by 8, the remainder is 7. Our new capacities are 8 and 7
3. When 8 is divided by 7, the remainder is 1. Our new capacities are 7 and 1.
4. When 7 is divided by 1, the remainder is 0. Our new capacities are 1 and 0. We stop here, concluding that the smallest amount we can leave in the basin is one cup.

8.4. The *backward* part of Euclid's algorithm

The method described in the previous section only tells us implicitly how to solve the original puzzle; it doesn't give us the precise equation telling us how many times to add or subtract the capacities of our initial containers. To find that equation, we proceed backwards through the calculations we have already done, performing a little algebra as we go.

As our first example, we revisit the last example of the previous section. Let's first re-examine the forward direction outlined there. Each time we come up with a new *artificial* container, we write an equation that shows how to achieve the capacity of the artificial container in terms of the two existing containers.

Forward calculations:

$$77 - 3 \cdot 23 = 8 \text{ so next we work with 23 and 8} \qquad (8.5)$$

$$23 - 2 \cdot 8 = 7 \text{ so next we work with 8 and 7} \qquad (8.6)$$

$$8 - 1 \cdot 7 = 1 \text{ so next we work with 7 and 1} \qquad (8.7)$$

The remainder when 7 is divided by 1 is 0, so we stop here.

The forward computation shows we can leave one cup in the basin. Let's derive an equation showing how.

Using our (artificial) 7-cup container and our (artificial) 1-cup container, it's easy:

$$1 = 0 \cdot 7 + 1 \cdot 1$$

We add 1 cup once and add 7 cups zero times. To get an equation showing how to leave 1 cup using an 8-cup container and a 7-cup container, we use Eq. (8.7) to substitute for the last 1 in the equation, the 1 that represents the capacity of our smallest artificial cup.

$$1 = 0 \cdot 7 + 1 \cdot (8 - 1 \cdot 7)$$

We use the distributive law to get

$$1 = 0 \cdot 7 + 1 \cdot 8 - 1 \cdot 1 \cdot 7$$

We collect the terms multiplying 7 to obtain

$$1 = 1 \cdot 8 + (0 - 1 \cdot 1) \cdot 7$$

Finally, we simplify the expression in parentheses, ending up with

$$1 = 1 \cdot 8 - 1 \cdot 7$$

(A lot of work to get an equation we already knew – but it illustrates the calculations needed for the subsequent steps.) We now have an equation showing how to leave 1 cup using an 8-cup container and a 7-cup container. Our 7-cup container is artificial, so we use Eq. (8.6) to substitute for the 7, getting

$$1 = 1 \cdot 8 - 1 \cdot (23 - 2 \cdot 8)$$

We use the distributive law to get

$$1 = 1 \cdot 8 - 1 \cdot 23 - 1 \cdot (-2) \cdot 8$$

We collect terms multiplying 8 to get

$$1 = -1 \cdot 23 + (1 + 2) \cdot 8$$

and simplify the expression in parentheses to get

$$1 = -1 \cdot 23 + 3 \cdot 8$$

We have an equation showing how to leave 1 cup using a 23-cup container and an 8-cup container. The 8-cup container is artificial, so we use Eq. (8.5) to substitute for the 8, obtaining

$$1 = -1 \cdot 23 + 3 \cdot (77 - 3 \cdot 23)$$

We collect the terms multiplying 23

$$1 = 3 \cdot 77 + (-1 + 3 \cdot (-3)) \cdot 23$$

and simplify, ending with

$$1 = 3 \cdot 77 - 10 \cdot 23$$

as our final equation.

Let's do one more example, this time with less explanation. We'll start with containers having capacities 876 and 524.

Forward calculations:

$$876 - 1 \cdot 524 = 352 \qquad\qquad (8.8)$$

$$524 - 1 \cdot 352 = 172 \qquad\qquad (8.9)$$

$$352 - 2 \cdot 172 = 8 \qquad\qquad (8.10)$$

$$172 - 21 \cdot 8 = 4 \qquad\qquad (8.11)$$

$$8 - 2 \cdot 4 = 0$$

and we stop here because the remainder is 0.

The number 4, the last number calculated before zero, is the greatest common divisor. Recall that because it is bigger than 1, we know that 524 has no mod-876 multiplicative inverse.

Backward direction:

$4 = 0 \cdot 8 + 1 \cdot 4$ Substitute for 4 using Eq. (8.11)
$\quad = 0 \cdot 8 + 1 \cdot (172 - 21 \cdot 8)$
$\quad = 1 \cdot 172 + (0 - 1 \cdot 21) \cdot 8$
$4 = 1 \cdot 172 - 21 \cdot 8$ Substitute for 8 using Eq. (8.10)
$\quad = 1 \cdot 172 - 21 \cdot (352 - 2 \cdot 172)$
$\quad = -21 \cdot 352 + (1 - 21 \cdot (-2)) \cdot 172$
$4 = -21 \cdot 532 + 43 \cdot 172$ Substitute for 172 using Eq. (8.9)
$\quad = -21 \cdot 352 + 43 \cdot (524 - 1 \cdot 352)$
$\quad = 43 \cdot 524 + (-21 + 43 \cdot (-1)) \cdot 352$
$4 = 43 \cdot 524 - 64 \cdot 352$ Substitute for 352 using Eq. (8.8)
$\quad = 43 \cdot 524 - 64 \cdot (876 - 1 \cdot 524)$
$\quad = -64 \cdot + (43 - 64 \cdot (-1)) \cdot 524$
$4 = -64 \cdot 876 + 107 \cdot 524$

8.5. The EuclidCards

Although the steps of Euclid's algorithm are pretty simple, it's easy to get confused. To help you carry out the steps, we have cards that guide you through. You would use one card for each forward step of the calculation.

The card looks like this:

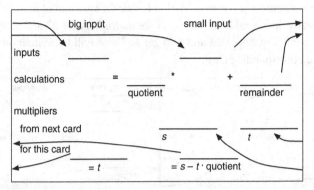

Near the top of the card, there are two blanks labeled *big input* and *small input*. You would write the capacities of the containers in these blanks (e.g., 77 and 23). In the next row, there are blanks where you would write the quotient (the big input divided by the small input) and remainder. This gives you one equation for the forward direction, e.g. $77 = 3 \cdot 23 + 8$ appears on the card as

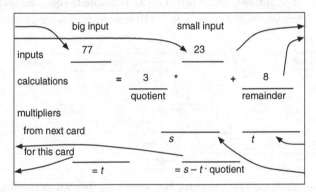

Notice the arrows going from the small input and the remainder off the right edge of the card. These arrows indicate that these two numbers should be copied onto another card; the new card's left edge should be attached to the old card's right edge so the arrows connect.

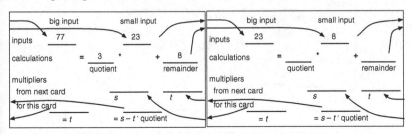

Now you are ready to find the quotient and remainder when 23 is divided by 8, thereby obtaining the second equation for the forward part of the calculation.

Eventually the calculation will yield the *multipliers* for 23 and 8, the numbers that need to multiply 23 and 8 to get 1. These will be written on the last row of the corresponding card.

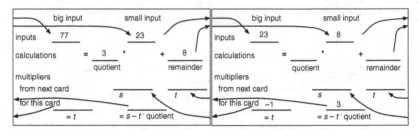

In this case, the multipliers for 23 and 8 are -1 and 3. You would copy these values into the blanks on the first card that are labeled s and t. Now you can derive the multipliers for 77 and 23 from the numbers s and t. The formulas are given on the cards: the multiplier for 77 is just t (which is 3), and the multiplier for 23 is $s - t \cdot quotient$, which is $(-1) - 3 \cdot 3$ because the quotient on the first card is 3. Thus you would write 3 and -10 into the blanks on the last row of the first card.

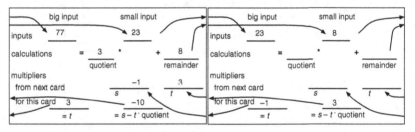

There is a special card for use in the last step of the forward calculation, when the small input is 0. The special card provides the multipliers, namely 1 and 0.

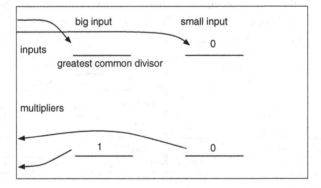

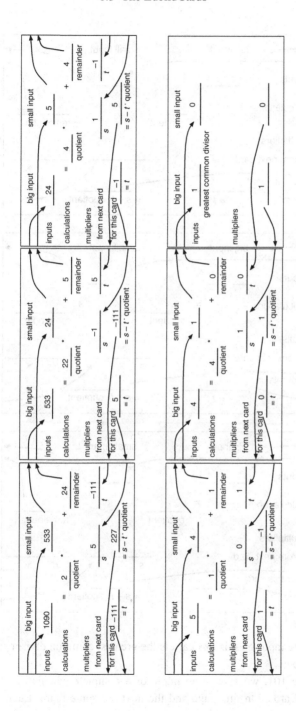

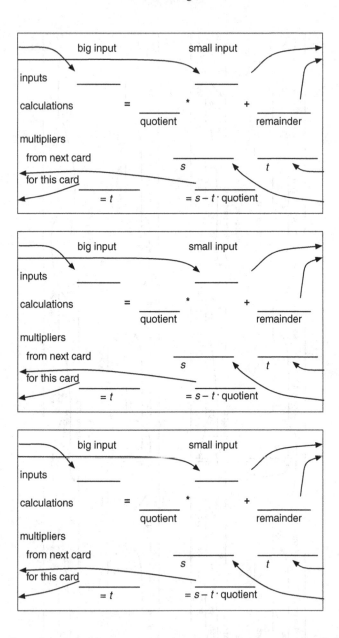

The large input on this last card is the greatest common divisor of the two original inputs.

On page 101, we give an example of a complete calculation done with the EuclidCards. On this page and the next are some blank EuclidCards to be copied for your use.

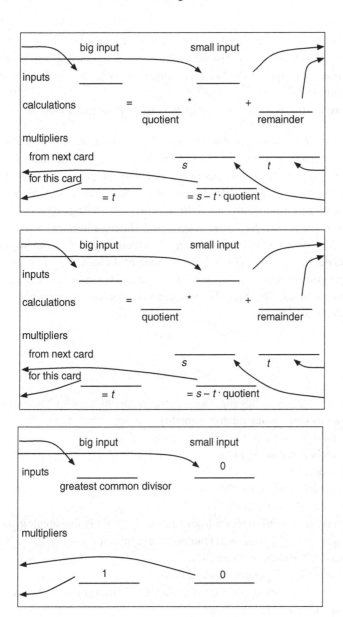

8.6. What Euclid's algorithm teaches us

We saw at the end of Section 8.3.1 that an integer b has a mod-a multiplicative inverse precisely when a and b are relatively prime. When this is true, moreover, Euclid's algorithm computes such a multiplicative inverse for us.

So what? As we saw back in Section 4.3.4 of Chapter 4, you could find multiplicative inverses for a particular modulus m by making a mod-m multiplication table for all mod-m representatives. What do we need Euclid's algorithm for?

There are two answers, one computational and one mathematical:

- *Computational need for Euclid's algorithm:* When m is a huge number, it is impractical to make the whole mod-m multiplication table. Euclid's algorithm provides a computational shortcut to computing a modular multiplicative inverse. In Chapters 13 and 14, we discuss cryptographic schemes that depend on computing multiplicative inverses for huge moduli.
- *Mathematical need for Euclid's algorithm:* Having a mathematical criterion for the existence of multiplicative inverses (namely relative primality) helps us to design cryptographic schemes. In the next chapter, we will introduce cryptographic schemes that depend on the existence of modular multiplicative inverses. We avoid the nonexistence problem by requiring that the modulus be a prime.

8.7. Problems

1. For each of the following, say whether a modular multiplicative inverse exists by considering relative primality.
   (a) mod-7 inverse of 6?
   (b) mod-7 inverse of 14?
   (c) mod-25 inverse of 4?
   (d) mod-25 inverse of 5?
   (e) mod-24 inverse of 21?
2. Recall Euler's phi function from Chapter 7. What is the smallest positive integer that has a mod-$\phi(21)$ multiplicative inverse?
3. Consider the integers 18 and 15.
   (a) What is the greatest common divisor?
   (b) Name two integers s and t such that the greatest common divisor equals $s \cdot 18 + t \cdot 15$.
4. Consider the integers 70 and 40.
   (a) What is the greatest common divisor?
   (b) Name two integers s and t such that the greatest common divisor equals $s \cdot 70 + t \cdot 40$.
5. Use EuclidCards on inputs 55 and 24. Find the greatest common divisor and integers s and t such that the greatest common divisor equals $s \cdot 55 + t \cdot 24$.

6. Use EuclidCards on 259 and 105. Find the greatest common divisor and integers s and t such that the greatest common divisor equals $s \cdot 259 + t \cdot 105$.
7. Use Euclid cards on 34 and 21. Find the greatest common divisor and integers s and t such that the greatest common divisor equals $s \cdot 34 + t \cdot 21$.
8. Use EuclidCards to find the mod-394820020 multiplicative inverse of 3.

9

Some Uses of Perfect Secrecy

It should be clear from Chapter 6 that perfect secrecy is useful in encryption. However, the idea can be useful in constructing other cryptographic building blocks. In this chapter, we discuss two examples.

9.1. Secret-sharing and perfect secrecy

The idea of perfect secrecy can be used to cryptographically "split" a secret into two parts. Each part can be given to a different person. Either person on her own learns nothing about the secret by receiving her part; together the two people can reconstruct the secret.

Imagine, for example, that the bank president wants to give her two vice presidents the combination to the safe (in case the safe needs to be opened on a day the president is incommunicado), but wants them to have only joint access. She can use secret-sharing to split the combination between the two vice-presidents.

Let $f(plain, key)$ be the encryption function for a perfectly secure cryptosystem. We will use this cryptosystem to split the secret. The choice of cryptosystem is not intended to be secret; we assume this choice is known to all. The choice of cryptosystem restricts the choice of secret to be shared; the secret must be one of the cryptosystem's possible plaintexts.

Let s be the secret to be shared. Choose a key k randomly and uniformly among all possible keys. The key k serves as the part to be provided to the first person. Encrypt s using the key k. The resulting cyphertext $f(s, k)$ serves as the part to be provided to the second person. Each part in itself provides no information on the secret: (1) the probability distribution of the key is uniform, regardless of the secret s, because that is the way the key was chosen, and (2) the probability distribution of the cyphertext is uniform, regardless of the secret s, because the cryptosystem is perfectly secure. However, the two people together can determine the secret; they decrypt the cyphertext with the key.

Example 6: Let m be any modulus, and consider the cryptosystem whose encryption function is

$$f(plain, key) = plain - key \quad (\text{mod } m)$$

Let s be a secret number between 0 and $m - 1$. For a random key k, the first part of the secret is k and the second part is the modulo-m representative of $s - k$. Thus the mod-m sum of the two parts is the secret.

The secret s can be split among any number of people. Suppose, for example, the secret must be shared among four people. Choose a random key k_1 and provide it to the first person. Let c_1 be the cyphertext resulting from encrypting the secret with key k_1. Now the secret c_1 must be shared among the three remaining people. Choose another random key k_2 and provide it to the second person. Let c_2 be the cyphertext resulting from encrypting c_1 with key k_2. Now s_2 must be shared among the remaining two people. Randomly choose a key k_3 and provide it to the third person. Finally, give the third person the cyphertext c_4 obtained by encrypting c_3 with the key k_3.

Example 6a: Using the cryptosystem of Example 6 to split the secret s among four people, the parts we end up with are four mod-m representatives whose mod-m sum is the secret s.

Of course, one can share a secret larger than any plaintext allowed by the cryptosystem: one simply breaks the secret up into blocks in the usual way (e.g., the first block is the first five symbols of the secret, and so on) and shares each of the blocks separately.

9.2. Threshold secret-sharing

The form of secret-sharing outlined above is fairly elementary. A more sophisticated and often more useful way to split up a secret among people is called *threshold secret-sharing*. Our bank president now has five vice presidents, and she needs to split the secret among them. However, she still wants to allow any two of them to be able to reconstruct the secret. We say in this case that the *threshold* is to be 2. Threshold secret-sharing allows her to split the secret among the five vice presidents in such a way that anyone alone cannot determine the secret, but any two can reconstruct it precisely. We use an equation for a line in modular arithmetic. In ordinary arithmetic, the equation for a line has the form

$$y = A \cdot x + B$$

That is, the set of pairs (x, y) of numbers satisfying this equation form a line. Ordinarily, A is called the *slope* of the line (it determines how steeply the line climbs), and B is called the *y-intercept* of the line (it is the position on the y-axis that the line intersects. (Note that the point $(0, B)$ is the intersection of the line with the y-axis.)

We will use the same idea, but combine it with modular arithmetic. Let's say our modulus m is a prime number (see Chapter 7) for reasons that will become apparent in later chapters. The equation for a line in modular arithmetic is

$$y \equiv A \cdot x + B \quad (\text{mod } m)$$

The "line" consists of the set of pairs (x, y) such that x and y are mod-m representatives and they satisfy the equation.

Because of modular arithmetic, such a line looks a little funny. For example, for a modulus m of 17, the line defined by

$$y \equiv 3 \cdot x + 5 \quad (\text{mod } 17)$$

is depicted in Figure 9.1.

Here's how to use a modular line to share a secret number. The modulus m is first chosen. Choose it to be big enough to exceed all possible secrets you might be sharing. We consider the modulus to be part of the system; it is public knowledge (recall the Kerckhoffs Doctrine). Next, secretly choose the slope A of the line uniformly at random among the mod-m representatives. Finally, let the y-intercept B be the secret number itself. To share the secret,

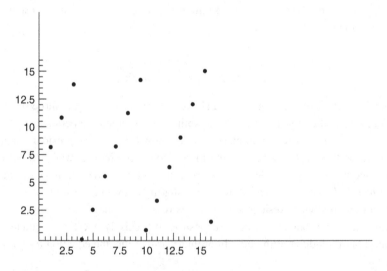

Figure 9.1. The line whose equation is $y \equiv 3 \cdot x + 5 \pmod{17}$.

give Vice President One the point $(1, A \cdot 1 + B)$, give Vice President Two the point $(2, A \cdot 2 + B)$, give Vice President Three the point $(3, A \cdot 3 + B)$, and so on.

First we discuss why a vice-president cannot by himself determine the secret. The only information he has been provided is a pair of mod m numbers (X, Y) where X is not zero. His goal is to determine the secret, which is the y-intercept of some line passing through his point (X, Y). However, there are lots of lines passing through his point. In fact, for every mod-m representative β, there is a line passing through (X, Y) whose y-intercept is β. Thus the one vice-president cannot by himself rule out any of the mod m numbers; based on what he knows, anyone of them could be the secret.

To prove this, we need only show that there is a line that passes through the two points $(0, \beta)$ and (X, Y). You may remember how to find the equation of a line passing through two points. Applying that formula, you would get the equation

$$y = ((Y - \beta)/X)x + \beta \qquad (9.1)$$

Using algebra, you can plug in the two points and verify that they both satisfy this equation. Thus there is indeed some line that passes through (X, Y) and has y-intercept β. This is true regardless of the value of β.

Let's try an example with a very small modulus, $m = 7$. Suppose the secret is 4. The bank president selects a random slope from among 0, 1, 2, 3, 4, 5, 6. Let's say she comes up with 2 for the slope. The equation of the line is then

$$y \equiv 2x + 4 \quad (\bmod\ 7)$$

Next she calculates points to give to her vice-presidents. For the first vice-president, she calculates the point $(1, 2 \cdot 1 + 4)$, which is $(1, 6)$. She then gives the first vice president the pair of numbers (1,6). She calculates the second vice president's point $(2, 2 \cdot 2 + 4)$, which is $(2, 1)$. (Remember, we are doing mod 7 arithmetic.) She therefore gives $(2, 1)$ to the second vice president. She calculates the third vice president's point $(3, 2 \cdot 3 + 4)$, which is $(3, 3)$. Similarly, the fourth vice president gets (4,5), and the fifth vice president gets $(5, 0)$.

Suppose the fourth vice president wants to try to figure out the combination by himself. (Of course, since our modulus is so small, he could just try all seven possibilities, but in practice the modulus would be too big for that.) He wants to find the equation of a line going through his point (4,5), for then he could figure out the y-intersect, which is the secret combination.

"Could the y-intersect be 0?" he wonders to himself. He refers to Eq. (9.1) to get the equation of a line going through (0,0) and (4,5), and finds that it is

$$y = (5/4)x + 0$$

Because we are doing arithmetic mod 7, the multiplicative inverse of 4 is 2 $(4 \cdot 2 = 1)$ so the value of $5/4$ is $5 \cdot 2$, which is 3. Thus he gets the equation

$$y = 3x + 0$$

He thinks to himself "this equation is indeed satisfied by the points $(0,0)$ and $(4,5)$, so maybe the y-intersect of the secret line is 0."

"Could the y-intersect be 11?" he wonders to himself. Again using Eq. (9.1), he obtains the equation

$$y = (4/4)x + 1$$

for an equation going through the points $(0,1)$ and $(4,5)$. He rewrites this equation as

$$y = 1x + 1$$

and realizes, "this equation is in fact satisfied by the points $(0,1)$ and $(4,5)$, so maybe the y-intersect of the secret line is 1."

"Could the y-intersect be 2?" He goes through the same procedure and ends up with the equation

$$y = 2x + 4$$

(This is the equation for the true secret line, but our rogue vice president doesn't know that.) He concludes that the secret might be 2.

"Could the y-intersect be 3? Could it be 4? Could it be 5? Could it be 6?" The vice president considers each of these possibilities in turn. For each, he manages to construct the equation for a plausible line, a line that goes through his point $(4,5)$ and that has the hypothesized y-intersect. He has convinced himself that 0, 1, 2, 3, 4, 5, and 6 are all possible y-intersects. Thus he has ruled out none of the possibilities: knowing his point has not helped him to learn anything about the secret.

Finally, we show that two vice presidents can together figure out the secret precisely. Two vice presidents together have two distinct points, so they can find the equation for the line that goes through these two points. Once they have that equation, they can look at it to determine the y-intersect.

For example, suppose vice presidents one and three legitimately come together to determine the secret. Vice president one has the point $(X_1, Y_1) = (1, 6)$, and vice president three has the point $(X_3, Y_3) = (3, 3)$. The slope of the line going through these two points is $(Y_1 - Y_3)/(X_1 - X_3)$, which is $(6 - 3)/(1 - 3)$. Now $6 - 3$ is 3, and $1 - 3$ is 5 (mod 7), so the slope is $3/5$. The multiplicative inverse of 5 is 3, so $3/5$ is $3 \cdot 3$, which is 2. They thus determine that the slope is 2. They now know the secret line's equation has the form

$$y = 2x + B$$

Because the line goes through their points, they can plug in one of them (say, the point $(1,6)$) to get

$$6 = 2 \cdot 1 + B$$

from which they can determine that the secret B is 4.

We have shown how to share a secret among many people so that any two can reconstruct the secret. The threshold for this scheme is said to be 2. The technique can be generalized to achieve any threshold desired. For example, suppose there are seven vice presidents, and the president wants any five of them to collectively be able to determine the secret. She would use a scheme with a threshold of 5. The same kind of calculations are used, but the specifics are beyond the scope of this text.

9.3. Message authentication codes

The same ideas as were used in threshold secret-sharing can be applied to the design of a message authentication code (MAC), a way of detecting changes to a message transmitted across an insecure channel.

Suppose Alice needs to send Bob a message. They don't care whether anybody reads the message (perhaps they have already encrypted it). However, they want to make sure that Bob gets the precise message sent by Alice. If they send the message across an insecure channel, they can't ensure that nobody tampers with the message, but they can take steps to recognize if it has been altered.

Suppose m is a prime number modulus that is larger than any message that might be sent. We assume consider m part of the system and therefore assume it is public. Suppose in addition that Alice and Bob have previously agreed upon a secret key, a pair of mod m numbers A and B selected uniformly at random. Nobody else knows the numbers A and B.

Now Alice wants to send the message X to Bob. She sends this message and also sends the value $Y = AX + B$, calculated mod m. Here Y is the message authentication code for the message X.

The message passes through a computer controlled by Eve. Eve therefore obtains the message X and the corresponding message authentication code Y. She may or may not choose to modify either of these before forwarding them to Bob. Let X^1 and Y^1 be the versions of the message and message authentication code she passes on to Bob.

Bob receives two numbers, the putative message X^1 and the putative message authentication code Y^1. To determine whether they are legitimate, he checks whether the pair (X^1, Y^1) lies on the line whose equation is

$$y = Ax + B$$

If not, he rejects them; they are not as Alice sent them. If they lie on that line, he assumes they are legitimate.

How can Eve cheat Bob? If she wants to alter the contents of the message (i.e., wants to send an X^1 that is different from X), she has to correspondingly alter the message authentication code so that Bob will accept the altered message. She has no idea, however, what the message authentication code should be for the altered message X^1.

All Eve knows about the secret line is that (X, Y) lies on that line. In order for her altered message/authentication-code pair (X^1, Y^1) to be accepted by Bob, she needs to ensure that this pair also lies on the line. What is the correct value of Y^1?

"Could the value be 0?" Eve asks. That would mean that the secret line passes through the points (X, Y) and $(X^1, 0)$. There is indeed such a line, so from Eve's perspective the correct value of Y^1 could very well be 0. "Could the value be 1?" There is a line passing through (X, Y) and $(X^1, 1)$, so, Eve thinks, perhaps the correct value of Y^1 is indeed 1. Similarly, any mod-m representative could be the correct value.

In fact, since A and B were chosen uniformly at random, it turns out that the value of Y^1 that Eve would need to use was effectively selected uniformly at random as well. Thus no matter how Eve guesses at Y^1, she has a probability of $1/m$ of guessing correctly. For a large value of m (say 10^{20}), this probability is so small as to be negligible. Eve wouldn't guess the right number even if she had millions of tries.

9.4. Problems

1. Each employee in your company has chosen a password for logging in to the computer system. Recently, your company has decided that each employee's password should be secret-shared among two other employees, just in case. Each password can be represented by a number from 0 to 9999. Your job is to choose the secret-sharing scheme. You can assume that the two employees holding shares of their co-worker's key will not collaborate to determine the key except in an official emergency. You consult with your three underlings, Larry, Moe, and Curly...

- Larry says:

  "For each secret password s to be shared, choose a random number b uniformly from 0 to 9999. The number b is the first share. Let $c = s - b$ (mod 10000). The number c is the second share."

- Moe says:

  "I agree with Larry's suggestion except for one thing. If the random number b is 0, the share c is the same as the secret. That's not very secure! I therefore propose that the number b be chosen uniformly from 1 to 9999 instead of from 0 to 9999."

- Curly says:

  "I agree with Moe's suggestion except for one thing. If the random number b is less than 10, then the share c will probably have the same hundreds place digit and the same thousands place digit as the secret s. That's not very secure! I therefore propose that the number b be chosen uniformly from 10 to 9999."

  Whose scheme is most secure, and why? Consider in particular how much the person receiving the share c thereby learns about the secret s.

2. In order that the secret combination to the CS007 safe would be available in an emergency situation, the TAs have each been given part of the secret. The secret consists of four mod-7 blocks. For each of these numbers, Prof. Klein chose a mod-7 line-the slope of the line is the secret number and the y-intercept was chosen randomly. Prof. Klein then provided each TA with an (x, y) point on each of the lines. Thus Kevin got a point on each of the four lines (namely the points with x-coordinate 1), Mark got a point on each of the four lines (namely the point with x-coordinate 2), and Sheryl got a point on each of the four lines (with x-coordinate 3). Due to a security slip-up, you happen on a few of the y-coordinates, as shown in the following table.

	1st block	2nd block	3rd block	4th block
Kevin ($x = 1$)	4	6		2
Mark ($x = 2$)	2		1	
Sheryl ($x = 3$)		3	1	

   (a) For each block of the secret that can be determined from the information given you, give us the block, showing your work.

   (b) For each block of the secret that cannot be determined from the information you have, tell us why it cannot be determined and tell us what possible values that block has.

3. You have seen the threshold secret-sharing scheme: each person who is supposed to share the key gets a point on a line and the secret is the y-intercept of that line. Say we have divided up the key among several people, and you and one other person have gotten together to combine your keys. Your point is $x = 4$ and $y = 8$, and your partner's point is $x = 5$ and $y = 0$. The modulus is 11. What is the secret?

4. In this problem we address the use of a MAC (message authentication code). The modulus for this problem is 11. Alice and Bob have previously agreed upon a secret key consisting of the two mod-11 numbers a and b. Thus the MAC function is

$$f(x) = ax + b$$

so when Alice sends a message X, she should accompany the message with the MAC $f(X)$.

If Alice and Bob had been paying attention, they would know that the MAC is secure only if the key is used once. Unfortunately, they missed this fact, and they send two distinct messages with MACs derived using the same key (the same pair of numbers a and b). You, Eve, intercept these messages and MACs:

message: 4, MAC: 5
message: 1, MAC: 9

You decide to tamper with the second message, changing it to 3. What MAC should accompany this forged message to convince Bob that it is legitimate?

5. Alice plans to send Bob a message accompanied by a MAC. (The method for generating the MAC is the one described in the text.) They have previously agreed on a uniformly random secret key for use with the MAC. The message will be sent in plaintext. The set of possible messages is $0, 1, \ldots, 12$ and the set of possible values of the MAC is also $0, 1, \ldots, 12$. Calculation of the MAC value is done modulo 13.

Eve plans to intercept the message and MAC, and send her own (fake) message, namely 12. She must also pick a fake MAC to accompany this message; her hope is to fool Bob into accepting the fake message as really being from Alice. She therefore needs to know the probability distribution for the MAC that should accompany the message 12 (i.e., if Alice were to send the message 12, what is the distribution of the MAC that would accompany that message?) Eve knows that the key for the MAC was chosen randomly and uniformly.

In each of the following scenarios, help Eve by sketching the distribution of the value of the MAC that should accompany her fake message.

(a) Eve must choose her fake MAC before seeing either the true message or the true MAC. Give the distribution of the MAC that would accompany the message 12.

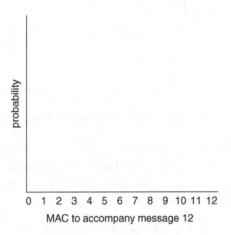

(b) Eve has intercepted the true message, 1, and the accompanying MAC, 2. Given what Eve now knows, sketch the distribution of the MAC that would accompany the message 12.

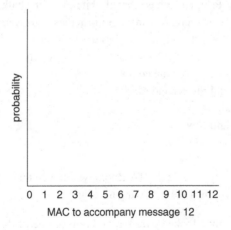

(c) Alice started to send the message 1 and the MAC 2, but changed her mind about the message and instead sent the message 2 and the MAC 4. Eve intercepted all this information. Given what Eve now knows, sketch the distribution of the MAC that would accompany message 12.

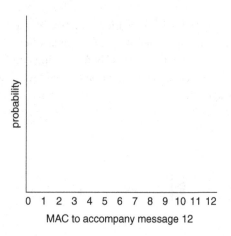

MAC to accompany message 12

6. Prof. Klein wants to provide the CS007 safe's combination to the teaching assistants using secret-sharing. The combination is known to be an eight-digit number. Prof. Klein chooses mod-10^8 numbers p, q, r, s, t so that they obey the following equations.

$$p + q \equiv \text{the safe's combination} \quad (\text{mod } 10^8)$$

$$r + s + t \equiv q \quad (\text{mod } 10^8)$$

$$r + q \equiv \text{the safe's combination} \quad (\text{mod } 10^8)$$

(Obviously, Prof. Klein has inhaled a bit too much chalk dust and has gotten confused about secret sharing.) He provides p to Kevin, q to Mark, r to Sandy, s to Sheryl, and, still confused, t to Kevin.

For each group of TA's given below, say whether or not the group can collectively figure out the combination.
(a) Sandy and Sheryl and Mark
(b) Kevin alone
(c) Sandy and Kevin
(d) Sheryl and Mark
(e) Sandy and Mark
7. (a) Wandering outside the TA Room, you notice that on the bulletin board in that room is the following message:

"Kevin: I looked over the midterm of one of the students. The student's score should be raised by 20 points. I have encrypted the initials of the student using a one-time pad with modulus 26: For each block,

$$cyph = plain + key \quad (\text{mod } 26)$$

The cyphertext is 10 12. The key will appear on a note I'll slip under the door. Signed, Sandy"

You see the piece of paper containing the key on the floor just inside the (locked) door.

It's folded, so you can't actually read the key. However, you decide to choose your own, fake key, write it on a similar piece of paper, and slide it under the door in the hope Kevin sees your piece of paper instead of Sandy's.

Can you come up with a key that would lead Kevin to add twenty points to your midterm score? If so, give such a key. If not, explain why not. Show your work.

(b) Now you are Kevin. You visit the TA Room and see the following message:

Kevin: Another student deserves a higher midterm score. Using the same encryption scheme as before, one-time pad with modulus 26, I've encrypted the initials of the student. The cyphertext is 17 23. To avoid the fiasco of last week, I've also calculated a MAC for each block of the *plaintext* using the formula

$$f(x) = Ax + B \text{ rem } 26$$

The MAC for the first block is 23, and the MAC for the second block is 7.

You see three folded-up sheets of paper with encryption keys written on them: "5 18," "12 20," and "19 0". You also see a sheet with a pair of MAC keys: "For first block, $A = 1, B = 25$, and for second block, $A = 1, B = 10$."

Assuming the MAC keys are correct, what is the correct plaintext?

10

Computational Problems, Easy and Hard

10.1. Computational problems

A computational problem is defined by specifying how the output is required to relate mathematically to the output. Here are some examples:

---

cube problem:

- *input:* integer b
- *output:* integer $b \times b \times b$

---

greatest common divisor problem:

- *input:* integers a, b
- *output:* greatest common divisor of a and b

---

modular cube problem

- *input:* modulus m, representative b
- *output:* representative c such that $c \equiv b \times b \times b \pmod{m}$

---

modular inverse problem

- *input:* modulus m, representative b
- *output:* representative c such that $c \cdot b = 1 \pmod{m}$, or "fail" if none exists.

---

modular exponentiation problem

- *input:* modulus m, representative b, positive integer k
- *output:* representative c such that

$$c \equiv \underbrace{b \times b \times \cdots \times b}_{k\text{times}} \quad (\text{mod } m)$$

An *instance* of a computational problem is an assignment of numbers to the inputs to the problem.

Example: an instance of the modular inverse problem is "the inverse of 160 modulo 937971"

10.2. Algorithms

An *algorithm* for a computational problem is a computational method, a procedure, that takes in the inputs and spits out an output that obeys the mathematical relation defined in the computational problem.

For example, we've learned two algorithms for the modular inverse problem, computing the mod-m multiplicative inverse of b. One involves writing out the mod-m multiplication table for mod-m representatives. The other is Euclid's algorithm.

10.2.1. The repeated-squaring algorithm for modular exponentation

Now consider the modular exponentiation problem: computing a mod-m representative for b^k. A naive algorithm simply starts with b and multiplies by b over and over, each time calculating the remainder when divided by m. After $k - 1$ multiplications, the result is b^k rem m.

The repeated squaring algorithm consists of two parts. In the first part, the algorithm starts with b, then multiplies it by itself ("squares" it) and takes the remainder, then squares the result and takes the remainder, and then squares that, and so on, a certain number of iterations. In the second part, the algorithm combines together some of these results, multiplying them together and taking the remainder. In order to make the algorithm more precise, we need the notion of binary expansion.

We ordinarily write numbers in base 10 ("decimal") notation. The rightmost digit is in the ones place, the second-to-rightmost digit is in the tens place, the third-to-rightmost digit is in the hundreds place, and so on. Thus 765 represents 7 times 10^2 plus 6 times 10^1 plus 5 times 10^0.

Another system for writing numbers is base 2 ("binary"), where the rightmost digit is in the ones place, the second-to-rightmost digit is in the twos place, the third-to-rightmost digit is in the fours place, the fourth-to-rightmost digit is in the eights place, and so on. Thus 100111 represents 1 times 2^5 plus 0 times 2^4 plus 0 times 2^3 plus 1 times 2^2 plus 1 times 2^1 plus 1 times 2^0, which is 39. The digits in binary notation are called "bits" (short for "binary digits"). By convention, the leftmost bit must be a 1 (just as ordinarily we don't write the number 7 as 007).

Back to the repeated-squaring algorithm. To calculate b^k rem m, we write k in binary. The position of the leftmost bit tells us how many squarings need to take place in the first part of the algorithm. For example, if the leftmost bit is in the 2^{11}'s place, then we need to calculate $b^{2^0}, b^{2^1}, b^{2^2}, b^{2^3}, \ldots, b^{2^{11}}$. Because the first number is just b, we need 11 squarings.

The ones in the binary representation of k tell us which powers of b that we have calculated we need to combine to get the final result. Here is an example, the multiplications needed to calculate b^{2184}. Next to each multiplication row, I have indicated an expression for the value calculated in that row.

NAME	COMMAND	value
result0	b	b^1
result1	result0 · result0	b^2
result2	resultl · resultl	b^4
result3	result2 · result2	b^8
result4	result3 · result3	b^{16}
result5	result4 · result4	b^{32}
result6	result5 · result5	b^{64}
result7	result6 · result6	b^{128}
result8	result7 · result7	b^{256}
result9	result8 · result8	b^{512}
resultl0	result9 · result9	b^{1024}
result11	resultl0 · result10	b^{2048}
finalresult	result3 · result7 · result11	b^{2184}

Say the exponent k takes L bits to represent. Then the number of multiplications for the first part of the algorithm is $L - 1$. In the second part of the algorithm, we need to multiply together some of the L results we obtained in the first part. Because we need to multiply together at most L values, we need at most $L - 1$ multiplications in the second part of the algorithm.

The number of bits needed to represent a positive integer k is 1 plus the rounded-down value of $\log_2 k$, (the base-2 logarithm of k). For example,

$\log_2 2184 = 11.092757\ldots$, so the rounded-down value of the logarithm is II. Thus this formula predicts that the number of bits needed to represent 2184 is 12. (For most purposes, it is good enough to neglect the "1 plus" and estimate the number of bits by $\log_2 k$.)

Similarly, the number of decimal digits needed to represent a number, say m, is 1 plus the rounded down value of the base-10 logarithm. for example, $\log_{10}765$ is $2.8836614\ldots$, so the rounded-down value is 2. Thus this formula predicts that the number of decimal digits to represent 765 is 3.

It is easy to convert between the base-10 log of a number and its base-2 log using the following formula. Memorize it!

$$\log_2 x \approx 3.3\log_{10} x$$

(The symbol $\approx$ denotes "is approximately equal to". For those who are curious about where the 3.3 comes from, this is the base-2 logarithm of 10.)

10.3. Predicting how many computer steps are needed by an algorithm

In order to predict how long a computer will take to execute an algorithm, we need a way to predict how long it will take to execute a single multiplication. Now the time per multiplication really should depend on how many digits are involved. For purposes of this book, we shall say therefore that the number of computer steps needed to multiply two numbers is the number of digits in whichever of the two numbers is larger.

We saw in Sections 2.6.2 and 2.7.3 of Chapter 2 that, in performing a series of multiplications, one can replace each intermediate result with a representative. In this way, we can ensure that we only multiply numbers that are less than the modulus. Thus our estimate for the number of computer steps required for a mod m multiplication is the number of decimal digits in m.

For example, the naive algorithm for calculating b^k (mod m) takes $k-1$ multiplications, all mod m. Because each multiplication takes roughly $\log_{10} m$ steps, the total number of computer steps is roughly $(\log_{10} m)(k-1)$.

The repeated-squaring algorithm for the same computational problem takes a number of multiplications that is at most twice the number of bits of k minus one. Because the number of bits of k is at most 1 plus the base- 2 logarithm of k, the number of multiplications is at most $2\log_2 k$. Each multiplication is done modulo m, and therefore takes at most $1+\log_{10} m$ computer steps. Thus the total number of computer steps for this algorithm is roughly $(\log_{10} m)(2\log_2 k)$.

10.4. Fast algorithms and slow algorithms, easy problems and hard problems

For small values of k, there is not much difference in number of computer steps between the naive algorithm and the repeated-squaring algorithm for the *modular exponentation problem*. However, as we increase k, the difference grows greater. Once k is a 100-digit number, we see from the formulae in the preceding section that there is a tremendous difference between the number of steps required by the naive algorithm and the number of steps required by the repeated-squaring algorithm. The first is considered a *slow* algorithm–it would take thousands of years to complete for l00-digit inputs. The repeated-squaring algorithm is considered a fast algorithm. Even for l000-digit inputs, a computer would complete the repeated-squared algorithm in a fraction of a second.

The naive algorithm for the *modular multiplicative inverse problem* involves constructing an $m \times m$ table, which requires about m^2 multiplications. This isn't too bad when m is 7 or 11. When it is a 100-digit number, it is completely impractical. By contrast, the number of cards required by Euclid's algorithm is about five times the number of decimal digits of m, and each card involves just one division, one multiplication, and one subtraction. Even on 1000-digit inputs, a computer would complete Euclid's algorithm in a fraction of a second.

In general, the distinction between fast and slow algorithms becomes clearer when the inputs become large – when the number of digits is in the hundreds or thousands. For this reason, it is helpful to have a formula in terms of input size for the number of computer steps required by an algorithm: it enables us to predict the amount of time the algorithm requires for large inputs.

To be useful, such a prediction need not be extremely accurate. The distinction between the two algorithms for modular exponentiation is so huge (when the input is large) that even if the number of steps required by each is underestimated or overestimated by a factor of a hundred, the distinction remains clear.

The distinction between fast and slow algorithms gives rise to the distinction between *easy* and *hard* computational problems. An *easy* computational problem is one for which there exists a fast algorithm. Thus modular exponentiation is considered an easy problem. A *hard* computational problem is one for which there is no fast algorithm. Note that we do not require that no fast algorithm is known – we require that none *exists*. Such a computational problem is *inherently* hard.

For many computational problems, we don't know whether they are easy or not: nobody has announced a fast algorithm but nobody has proved that no fast algorithm exists. Often we resort to making the assumption that a computational problem is hard if algorithms researchers have unsuccessfully tried to find a fast algorithm for it. We will see an example of such a *presumably* hard computational problem in the next chapter.

10.4.1. Computational problems and cryptography

Why do we care about whether a computational problem is easy or hard? In previous chapters, we saw cryptographic schemes (such as the one-time pad) that release no information at all if used properly. However, achieving this kind of security is sometimes difficult in practice. Many other schemes are based on the dichotomy between easy problems and hard problems. For example, we would like an encryption scheme that would enable use to perform many encryptions with a single key; we want encryption and decryption to be easy for someone who knows the key, but we want cracking (decryption without the key) to be hard.

In the next chapter, we explore cryptographic schemes whose security relies on the dichotomy between any easy problem (modular exponentiation) and a problem that is *believed* to be hard.

10.5. Problems

1. Suppose the number c has n digits and the number d has m digits. For each of the following, give a formula in terms of m and n.
   (a) Roughly how many digits does $1000 \cdot c$ have?
   (b) Roughly how many digits does $c + d$ have?
   (c) Roughly how many digits does $c \cdot d$ have?
   (d) Roughly how many digits does $c \cdot d^2$ have?

2. The DigiComp computer can add a pair of digits (and a carry, if needed) in one clock tick. Thus, to add two 10-digit numbers, DigiComp requires ten ticks. To add a 10-digit number and a 6-digit number, DigiComp takes six or seven ticks (depending on the final carry). For each of the given addition problems, tell us how many clock ticks DigiComp needs to solve the problem. Your answer need not be exact; it's okay to be off slightly.
   (a) 12345678
       + 1234

(b) 123456789012345678
     + 123456789012345

(c) 1234567890123456789012345678901234567890
     + 1234567890123456789012345678901234567890

(d) 123456789
     234567891
     + 345678912

(e) 12345678901234567890
     23456789012345678901
     34567890123456789012
     45678901234567890123
     56789012345678901234
     67890123456789012345
     78901234567890123456
     89012345678901234567
     90123456789012345678
     +
     ----

3. The DigiComp computer can multiply a pair of digits (and add in a carry, if
    needed) in one clock tick. Thus to multiply a 20-digit number by a 1-digit
    number, DigiComp requires 20 ticks. Multiplying a 20-digit number by a
    2-digit number, say 37, involves (i) multiplying the 20-digit number by 7,
    obtaining a 20- or 21-digit number, (ii) multiplying the 20-digit number
    by 3, obtaining a 20- or 21-digit number, and shifting it to the left by one
    place, and (iii) adding the results of (i) and (ii). Part (i) takes 20 ticks, part
    (ii) takes 20 ticks, and part (iii) takes about 21 ticks. Thus the total number
    of ticks required is about 61.

       For each of the following multiplication problems, tell us how many
    clock ticks DigiComp needs to solve the problem. Show your work.
    (Your answer need not be exact; there is no problem with being off by
    a few.) **Don't be afraid to use short-cuts; i.e. if you think you see a
    pattern, use it.**

(a) 12345678
     $\times$ 123

(b) 12345
     $\times$ 1234

(c) 1234567890123456789012345678901234567890
     $\times$ 1234567890
     ----

4. Suppose DigiComp needs to multiply two k-digit numbers. Which formula below most accurately expresses the number of ticks needed? Explain your answer by referring to the multiplication process. **Note: The formula you choose need not be exactly correct, it need only be the best estimate. The percentage error for the correct formula is smaller for larger values of k, while the percentage error for incorrect formulae tend to be larger for larger values of k. You can check your answer by seeing how accurately the formula you choose predicts the number of ticks required for multiplying, say, two 10-digit numbers. As in the previous problem, don't be afraid to use short-cuts: look for patterns.**
   - $k+2$
   - $4k$
   - $2k\sqrt{k}$
   - $2k^2$
   - $k^3/8$
   - 2^k
   - $10^k - 2$

5. For each of the following formulae, imagine a computer for which that formula gave the number of ticks required to multiply two k-digit numbers. For which values of k would DigiComp be faster, and for which values of k would the imaginary computer be faster? Your answer need not be exact. **Hint: you may find it helpful to graph the functions.**
   (a) $10k+4$
   (b) $k^2\sqrt{\sqrt{k}}$
   (c) $2^k/1100$
   (d) $2^{\sqrt{k}}$

6. The base-10 logarithm of a number is roughly the number of digits comprising that number. Use this fact to estimate the base-10 logarithms given below. (Don't use a calculator.)

    (a) $\log_{10} 12345678901234567890$

    (b) $\log_{10} 1234567890123456789012345678901234567890123456789012$
        34567890

    (c) $\log_{10} 9999999999999$

    (d) $\log_{10} 1111111111111$

7. For each of the following, give a value of x for which the base-10 logarithm is approximately the number given. (There are many right answers.)

    (a) $\log_{10} x \approx 5$

    (b) $\log_{10} x \approx 7$

    (c) $\log_{10} x \approx 30$

8. Suppose DigiComp needs to multiply the numbers a and b. Which of the following formulae most accurately estimates the number of ticks required to perform the multiplication? Explain your answer, and compare it to the exact answer for $a = 1234567890, b = 1234567890$.

    • a/b

    • $4a^2b^2$

    • $2\log_{10} ab$

    • $2(\log_{10} a)(\log_{10} b)$

    • $10^a 10^b$

9. Another imaginary computer requires approximately k^3 clock ticks to multiply two k-digit numbers. Which of the following formulae must accurately estimates the number of ticks this computer requires to multiply the numbers a and b? Explain your answer, and compare it to the exact answer for $a = 1234567890, b = 1234567890$.

    • a^3b^3

    • $(ab)^3$

    • $(10^a 10^b)^3$

    • $(\log_{10} a)^3(\log_{10} b)^3$

    • $\log_{10} (a^3b^3)$

10. (a) For each of the following numbers given in binary, give the decimal representation, showing how you obtained your answer.

    i. 101

    ii. 1111

    iii. 10100111010

(b) For each of the following numbers given in decimal, give the binary representation, showing how you obtained your answer.

i. 7

ii. 16

iii. 632

11. For each of the following numbers x, estimate $\log_{10} x$. Your answer need not be exact. We ask only that your answer be an integer within 1 of the correct answer. We also request that you not use a calculator for this.

   (a) 865733500

   (b) 3257100392479038

   (c) 2903483223973759397330024

   (d) 440956638333799740905525263563

12. For each of the following numbers x, estimate $\log_2 x$. Again, your answer need not be exact. We ask only that your answer be an integer within 1 of the correct answer. We also request that you not use a calculator for this.

   (a) 75777 (decimal)

   (b) 3337150 (decimal)

   (c) 10111011001 (binary)

   (d) 10101010000011111111010(binary)

13. We showed the operations needed to do modular exponentiation using a table like the one below, which shows how to calculate b^{2184} modulo some unspecified number. You should interpret each multiplication as being done with respect to the unspecified modulus.

NAME	COMMAND	formula for value computed
result0	b	b^1
result1	result0 · result0	b^2
result2	result1 · result1	b^4
	⋮	⋮
result12	result11· result11	b^{2048}
finalresult	result3· result7 · resultl2	b^{2184}

For each of the exponentials below, first obtain the binary expansion for the exponent, showing your work. Notice how many bits are needed in your binary expansion. Next, prepare a table very much like the one above indicating the operations needed to calculate the exponential. Your table should have one row for each bit of the exponent's binary expansion, plus one additional row for multiplying together the appropriate results to obtain the desired final result. Finally, count up the number of multiplications needed by the calculation you propose.

(a) b^{16}

(b) b^{128}

(c) b^{257}

(d) b^{194}

14. You will need a calculator for this problem. In this problem, we let two computers, MegaComp and SlowThink, compete head on head. Our "racetrack" is the calculation of $b^{938115730327217}$ modulo 3068862310548665. Note that the exponent and the modulus are 15-digit numbers.

    MegaComp is very fast and very dumb. Its designers didn't know about the repeated squaring method, so it uses the naive method for calculating modular exponentials. (Recall the formula for the number of operations required for this algorithm.) However, MegaComp performs a million (1,000,000) steps per second.

    SlowThink is very slow. It was designed in an earlier era, and performs only a thousand steps per second. However, it uses the repeated squaring method for calculating modular exponentials.

    Start your computers at the sound of the gun....

    (a) How long will MegaComp take to complete its calculation of the exponential mentioned above. *Hint: Your answer may be best expressed in years.*

    (b) Give a good overestimate of how long SlowThink will take.

11

Modular Exponentiation, Modular Logarithm, and One-Way Functions

11.1. Modular logarithms

As we mentioned at the end of the last chapter, cryptography exploits the dichotomy between easy computational problems and hard computational problems. We saw in that chapter that the following computational problem is easy: even for input numbers with hundreds of digits, a computer can calculate the output in a reasonable amount of time.

---

modular exponentiation problem

- *input:* modulus m, representative b, positive integer k
- *output:* mod-m representative c such that

$$c \equiv \underbrace{b \times b \times \cdots \times b}_{k \text{ times}} \pmod{m}$$

We next give an example of a computational problem that is believed to be hard.

---

modular logarithm problem

- *input:* modulus m, mod-m representative b, representative c
- *output:* nonnegative integer k such that $b^k \equiv c \pmod{m}$ if such an integer exists; otherwise, the answer "none exists".

If there exists an integer k such that $b^k \equiv c \pmod{m}$, we say that k is a mod-m-logarithm (base b) of c. In this book, we sometimes write this mathematically as

$$k = \text{mod} m \log_b c$$

This notation is deceptive in that it suggests that mod$m$ log$_b$ is a function. In fact, as our description of the computational problem indicates, there is sometimes no modular logarithm for a given m, b, and c. Moreover, Euler's Theorem (described in the chapter on number theory) can be used to show that if there is a modular logarithm, there are an infinite number. Suppose k is the mod m logarithm base b of c. This means that

$$b^k \equiv c \pmod{m}$$

By Euler's Theorem, as long as b is relatively to prime to m,

$$b^{\phi(m)} \equiv 1 \pmod{m}$$

Multiplying these two equations, we get

$$b^k b^{\phi(m)} \equiv c \pmod{m}$$

Finally, using the first law of exponentiation, we get

$$b^{k+\phi(m)} \equiv c \pmod{m}$$

That is, $k + \phi(m)$ is also a mod m logarithm base b of c.

Thus mod$m$ log$_b$ fails to be a function in two ways: for some inputs, it has no answers and for some inputs it has many answers. Nevertheless it is often useful to view it as a function. We can get away with this behavior because, in many cases where it arises, (1) we know from the start that there is some answer, and (2) it doesn't matter which answer we get.

11.1.1. How modular logarithms differ from ordinary logarithms

The modular logarithm seems to resemble the ordinary, nonmodular logarithm. The ordinary base-b logarithm of c is defined to be the real number x such that $b^x = c$. This equation reminds one of the (modular) equation defining the modular logarithm. Moreover, like the modular logarithm, an ordinary logarithm question sometimes has no answer (when the input c is nonpositive). You can calculate ordinary logarithms on a scientific calculator, at least base-10 logarithms. Why should the modular logarithm problem be difficult when the ordinary logarithm problem is so easy that a calculator can solve it?

The answer seems to have something to do with approximation. A calculator typically isn't calculating an exact logarithm; it's calculating an approximate logarithm. For example, my calculator tells me that the base-10 logarithm of 17 is 1.2304489 but when I test this answer by raising 10 to the power of 1.2304489, my calculator tells me the answer is not 17 but 16.999999. In fact, the base-10 logarithm of 17 can't be represented exactly using a finite number of digits. Why am I satisfied with a calculator that gives me a wrong answer? The fact that 10 to the power of 1.2304489 is very close to 17 tells me that in fact the base-10 logarithm of 17 is very close to 1.2304489. Thus the answer my calculator gives me is very close to the exact answer. Moreover, because 10 to the power of 1.2304489 is smaller than 17, we can conclude that 1.2304489 is smaller than the exact base-10 logarithm of 17. These kinds of observations were used to formulate a good algorithm for calculating a good approximation to a logarithm.

Contrast this situation with that arising in modular arithmetic. Let the modulus m be 97330327. what is the base-2 logarithm of 88319671? That is, we want to calculate the number k such that

$$2^k \equiv 88319671 \pmod{97330327}$$

By trying different exponents, I happened across the exponent 28305819, which leads to a different but similar number:

$$2^{28305819} \equiv 88032151 \pmod{97330327}$$

This suggests that 28305819 might be a good approximation to the log of 88319671. Also, since the result of exponentiating to the power of 28305819 has a representative smaller than 88319671, one might be tempted to guess that 28305819 is smaller than the exact logarithm of 88319671.

In fact, the true logarithm is 12314, which is very different from our guess of 28305819 and is smaller than it. We conclude that, in modular arithmetic in contrast to ordinary arithmetic, just because two numbers are close does not mean their logarithms are close.

It is also true that the value of a number's modular logarithm generally has no resemblance to the value of that number's ordinary logarithm. For example, the ordinary base-2 logarithm of 88319671 is roughly 26.396231. It is only very rarely that the modular logarithm equals the ordinary logarithm. (This happens when the ordinary logarithm is exact and is so small than the base to that logarithm is still smaller than the modulus. For example, the ordinary base-2 logarithm of 16384 is precisely 14; because 16384 is smaller than the modulus 97330327, the modular base-2 logarithm of 16384 is also 14.)

11.1.2. Modular exponentiation as a one-way function

A one-way function is a function f such that the first problem below is computationally "easy" and the second problem is computationally "hard".

forward: Input: an element b of the domain of f.
Output: the value of $f(b)$.
backward: Input: an element c of the range of f.
Output: an element b of the domain of f such that $f(b) = c$

Thus a one-way function is one for which it's easy to go from a domain element to its image, but hard to go from a range element to its pre-image.

It is important to realize that a one-way function does not involve a key. It can be assumed that the details of the one-way function are known to everybody, including potential hackers. The security of a system that uses one-way functions should not depend on any mystery surrounding the one-way function but only on the computational difficulty of going backwards.

Our example of a one-way function is $f(x) = 2^x \pmod{m}$, where m is a huge odd modulus, say a couple hundred digits. For an input b, a computer can use the repeated-squaring algorithm to calculate $y = 2^b \pmod{m}$ in a few hundred thousand steps – no problem. However, to calculate b from the value y is to solve the modular logarithm problem. We believe that there is no good algorithm for this problem.

Of course, this does not mean that every instance of the backward problem is hard to solve. We have seen in this book, for example, that if the modulus m is very small, finding the modular logarithm is not hard. Even if the modulus m is huge (as it should be), if the value of b is very small then $2^b \pmod{m}$ is the same as 2^b – it's as if we're doing the exponentiation in ordinary arithmetic because the numbers don't get big enough for the modular nature of the arithmetic to have any effect. For such an instance, going backwards involves taking an ordinary (exact) logarithm. This apparent security flaw is subsumed by a more general issue concerning the use of one-way functions. The more general issue arises in both example applications we discuss below.

For some applications, f being one-way is not sufficient. In discussing the second of two applications below, we see that modular exponentiation has at least one weakness that makes it not quite suitable; there is a kind of security defect. In this book, we are ignoring this defect. Use of modular exponentiation as a one-way function also has a usability defect: even though we have a reasonably fast algorithm for modular exponentiation, the *repeated squaring* algorithm, for some applications even this is not fast enough. For these two reasons, in practice other, more complicated functions are used as one-way functions.

11.1.3. Security parameter

We have said that the distinction between easy and hard computational problems becomes more pronounced as the input size grows. Thus the bigger the input size, the greater the security. The disadvantage of large input size, however, is that it impairs usability; the time required for even a fast algorithm grows as the input size increases.

In order to allow the user of a cryptographic scheme to decide how to balance this tradeoff, therefore, a typical cryptographic scheme comes with

user	password
Aaron	"bubble gum"
Alice	"mosquito"
Anselm	"cat"
⋮	⋮
Zachary	"mosquito"

Figure 11.1. In a straightforward approach to organizing the password file, each entry gives the password of one user.

a "dial" called the *security parameter*. The higher the security parameter, the more secure the scheme but also the less convenient for those using the scheme. For the exponential one-way function, the security parameter is the number of decimal digits in the modulus m.

11.2. Application of one-way functions to password security

Consider the use of passwords for restricting access to some resource such as a computer. In a straightforward approach, the computer stores a big table called the *password file*. Each user is listed in the table along with that user's password. When someone tries to gain access (by logging in), they give their name and password to the computer, and the computer looks up the name in the table and compares the password given to the one recorded in the table under that name. If they match, the computer assumes that the person trying to log in gave their real name, and grants the person access.

In such a system, the password file is a weak point in the security of the system. A hacker who somehow manages to gain access to the password file immediately obtains the password of every user of the system and can henceforth impersonate every user. Since people often use the same password for access to multiple systems, this sometimes enables the hacker to break into other computer systems, and so on. This trick was one of those used by the Internet Worm of November 1988, a rogue program that duplicated itself and spread broadly through the Internet.

To make the password file slightly less useful to hackers, a one-way function is used. Along with the name of each user, instead of giving the user's password, the table gives the image of the password under the one-way function. Now when a user tries to log in, supplying her name and password to the system, it applies the one-way function to the password, obtaining the image of the password under that function, and compares that result to the user's entry in the password file. If there is a match, the user is granted access.

user	f (password)
Aaron	29510086573
Alice	7792389588043
Anselm	193837727847
⋮	⋮
Zachary	7792389588043

Figure 11.2. In a more secure system, each entry of the password file gives the image of the user's password under a fixed one-way function f. In this example, f("bubble gum") = 29510086573 and f("mosquito") = 7792389588043. Note that the same value is stored under Alice's name and Zachary's name because they happen to have chosen the same password.

How does this use of a one-way function enhance security? A hacker who gains access to the password file does not thereby obtain passwords for all the users, at least not directly. The definition of a one-way function (namely the fact that it is computationally difficult to "go backwards") implies that the hacker cannot easily derive a user's password from the corresponding value stored in the password file.

11.2.1. Dictionary attack on password files that use a one-way function

Use of a one-way function with a password file does not eliminate the risks associated with a hacker getting her hands on the password file. Because they need to remember their passwords, users tend to choose common words or names as passwords. A hacker could prepare a list of ten thousand or so commonly used passwords (e.g., a dictionary). She could then apply the one-way function to each of them, and see if the resulting values appear in the password file. Each match gives her the password of a user.

One might argue that the hacker could try out each of the words in the dictionary by simply trying to log in. (This is the view of hacking presented in the movie *War Games*.) After all, this attack does not require the hacker to access the password file. There are three reasons why this attack is likely to be much less effective than one involving the password file First, a good computer system incorporates a delay into the log-in procedure: the user is forced to wait a few seconds between successive attempts to log in. Consequently it is infeasible to tryout thousands of different passwords. In contrast, the hacker can test tens of thousands of potential passwords each second against a password file. Second, after some user has made numerous unsuccessful attempts to log in, system administrators are alerted that an attempt to break in may be underway.

user	salt	f (salt • password)
Aaron	573951212	998778673
Alice	8200294838	485823992
Anselm	784389387	2948872387
⋮	⋮	⋮
Zachary	84390239854	686723745

Figure 11.3. In a still more secure system, a salt is selected for each user, and the one-way function is applied to a combination of the salt and the password. Note that the output of the one-way function is different for Alice and Zachary even though they have the same password.

Third, this attack requires that the hacker try each password separately with each user name; according to what we have seen so far, the hacker with access to the password file can apply the one-way function to a potential password just once and then quickly see if the resulting value occurs anywhere in the password file.

11.2.2. Salting the password file

This last observation concerning the effectiveness of a dictionary attack on the password file suggests a technique to hinder a hacker's attack. The goal is to ensure that each entry in the password file is specific to the user. When a user's password is to be entered into the system, an additional number, called the salt, is chosen. The salt may depend on the user's name, or on the time of day the password is to be entered-anything that is likely to vary from user to user. The input to the one-way function is obtained by combining the password with the salt. As usual, the corresponding output of the one-way function is stored in the password file under the user's name. The salt is also stored along with the output.

When the user later tries to log in and supplies her name and password, the system looks up the user's name in the password file and determines the corresponding salt. The system then combines the salt with the password provided by the user, and applies the one-way function to the combination. The system compares the result to the value stored in the password file.

11.3. Application of one-way functions to logging in: s/key

As discussed in Chapter 1, while in Rhode Island I can remotely log on to a computer in California by sending my password through the Internet.

This method is clearly not secure: an eavesdropper who controls one of the intermediate computers can record my password and computer account name. One long-ago product for addressing this insecurity was s/key.

The s/key system uses a one-way function f. To use s/key, I first choose a secret key-let's say it's a 20-digit number s. I then use an s/key computer program to find the image of s under the one-way function f, and then the image of that image, and the image of that image and so on, perhaps 100 times. The resulting value can be written as

$$\underbrace{f(f(f(\cdots(f(s))\cdots)))}_{100 \text{ times}}$$

We abbreviate this as $f^{100}(s)$.

I would then provide this value to the California computer, and it would store the value for my future log-ins.

Later, when I want to log in to the California computer, it would ask me for the pre-image of the value it has saved for me. Note that the pre-image of $f^{100}(s)$ is $f^{99}(s)$ because

$$f^{100}(s) = f(f^{99}(s))$$

Because I know s, I can reconstruct the value of $f^{99}(s)$ by running an s/key program, and I send it to the California computer. The California computer checks if the value I sent is really the pre-image of the value it had stored. How can it do that? It can't calculate the pre-image of the stored value because that would take too long f is a one-way function. Instead, it finds the image of the value I sent, and compares it to the stored value. Once it verifies that the numbers match, it stores the new value, the value I sent it, for next time.

The next time I try to log in to the California computer, it asks me for the pre-image of $f^{99}(s)$, so I send it $f^{98}(s)$. Thus I am able to log in 100 times before I am forced to re-initialize the system by choosing a new secret key s.

This system is more secure than one in which I must send my password over the network: By the time an eavesdropper sees my response to the California computer's question, my response has made it to the California computer, and I have logged in. The value with which I responded is no longer useful for logging in; next time, the computer wants a different value before granting access: in particular, it wants the pre-image of the value it last saw. The eavesdropper can't calculate that pre-image because the function is one-way.

Note that the California computer does not store any secret information; I retain the only copy of the secret s. That way, not even someone with privileged access to the files on the California computer could log in as me.

11.4. (Mis) application of one-way functions to commitment

I write a secret on a piece of paper, seal it in an envelope, and hold the envelope in front of your eyes. At this point,

concealing: You don't yet know what is written on the paper, and
binding: I cannot change what I have written on the envelope without you noticing.

At some later point, I hand you the envelope and you can determine my secret.

The preceding scenario is the model for a commitment protocol, a basic element in cryptographic applications. It arises in a surprising variety of settings. The first stage of the protocol is the *commit* stage. The second stage, in which I make it possible for you to learn the secret, is called *decommitment* (this is a terrible choice of term). Between the first and second stage, typically you make some kind of decision and announce your decision to me. The *concealing* property of the commitment protocol ensures that you cannot base your decision on my secret, and the *binding* property of the protocol ensures that I cannot change my secret based on your announced decision.

How can commitment be implemented digitally? That is, how can the same functionality be achieved if you and I are on opposite sides of the earth, and are connected by the Internet? Perhaps the method that most readily comes to mind involves encryption. For the commit stage, I choose a random key, encrypt my secret with that key, and send you the cyphertext. For the decommit stage, I send you the key, allowing you to decrypt the cyphertext.

The problem with this approach to implementing commitment is that at least some encryption schemes are not binding. That is, they don't reliably prevent me from changing my secret once I hear your decision. The problem is that the choice of key gives me an extra little control over what you get when you decrypt. I can choose which key to give you depending on your decision. This problem is particularly troublesome if the encryption scheme is the one-time pad: even after I've sent you the cyphertext, I am not bound to any particular secret, since by an appropriate choice of the key I provide you I can make the cyphertext decrypt to whatever I want.

This example demonstrates that when we use encryption to implement commitment, there is a conflict between the two goals of commitment, the concealing property and the binding property. Use of a perfectly secure encryption scheme ensures that the concealing property holds and the binding property does not hold. However, there are encryption schemes that can be used (in conjunction with another trick) to achieve both properties.

In this chapter, our solution will be to do without keys, thereby avoiding the additional freedom provided to me by the choice of keys. A one-way function is a way to conceal without keys. A basic (and, as we will see, flawed) implementation of commitment using a one-way function f is as follows. (Remember that we agree on the protocol in advance, including the choice of one-way function.)

- To commit to my secret s, I calculate $c = f(s)$ and send the result c to you.
- To decommit, I simply send you my secret s. You check that I have not lied by calculating $f(s)$ and checking that it matches the value c I sent you in the commit stage.

This implementation seems to realize both properties of commitment. Because f is a one-way function, knowing the value c does not enable you to determine s. Because I have already sent you the value of f(s), I cannot later change my mind and send you an alleged secret that differs from s.

In fact, both these inferences are fallacious, and under some circumstances the above protocol is neither concealing nor binding. However, by making some slight changes we can achieve both these properties.

11.4.1. Not concealing

The reason the straightforward implementation is not concealing is related to the dictionary attack discussed in the context of password security. Very often the set of possible secrets is a relatively small set. Once you have received $c = f(s)$ from me, you can try all possible secrets, applying f to each one and checking whether the corresponding output matches c. In this way, you can learn something about the secret before the decommit stage.

Suppose, for example, you know in advance that my secret is either 0 or 1. This is a frequent case in applications and is called "bit commitment" because I am committing to a single bit. If I were to send you $c = f(s)$, you could simply calculate $f(0)$ and $f(l)$ and see which one yields c as a result.

More generally, as in the case of passwords, even if the range of possible secrets is large, you might have some knowledge about the choice of secrets I am likely to make. If there is a small subset of possible secrets that you suspect I might select among, you can try each of these likely candidates. Of course, your suspicion might be incorrect: I might have chosen none of these. However, if there is a nonnegligible chance that your suspicion is accurate, we should consider the security to be undermined.

For example, consider a number-guessing game. Let us assume that any number from 1 to 10^{10} is allowed. I commit to my guess, then you reveal your number, and then I reveal my guess. I win if my guess is within 10^7 of your number. Can you figure out my guess before I reveal it? In principle, once you have the commitment $c = f(\text{my guess})$, you could try all 10^{10} possible numbers, applying f to each one and comparing the result to c. You might feel disinclined to do all that work. However, if you knew that I might have a preference for guessing the birthdates of friends, you could with little work have a reasonable shot at determining my guess. In some applications even a reasonable shot gives you a substantial advantage.

In a sense, the problem is that there is not enough unpredictability in my secret. To remedy the problem, more randomness is needed in the protocol. Here is the improved protocol.

- I choose a big random number r (called a *nonce*) to be used only for this one occasion. I combine r with my secret s, obtaining a new number k, such that anyone who knows k can figure out s from it.
- To commit to my secret, I calculate $c = f(k)$ and send the result c to you.
- To decommit, I send you the number k. You can derive my secret s from k. You can also check that I have not lied by calculating $f(k)$ and checking that it matches the value c I sent you in the commit stage.

Before I decommit, you have no idea what nonce I chose. Because there are so many possibilities for the nonce and therefore so many possibilities for the combined number k, you cannot try all possibilities: it would take you too long. Thus this modified protocol seems to be secure against the kind of attack we have considered.

By what formula should the numbers s and k be combined? The precise method of combining is not so important as long as both parties, you and I, agree in advance on the method so there is no confusion (intended or otherwise) as to my secret once you know k. For purposes of this book, an easy and reasonably effective way of combining is as follows. Suppose the secret is guaranteed to be a nonnegative number less than T. (In the bit-commitment example, $T = 2$ and in the number-guessing example, $T = 10^{10} + 1$.) The value of T is agreed upon in advance; it is considered part of the protocol and is therefore known to all parties. One can combine the nonce r with the secret s using the formula

$$k = r \cdot T + s$$

It follows from elementary number theory that because s is nonnegative and less than T, the remainder when k is divided by T is s. That is, s is the mod-T representative of k.

11.4.2. Not binding

The reason our implementation of commitment is not binding is that the one-way function need not be one-to-one. Suppose, for example, that our one-way function is $f(x) = 2^x$ (mod 660761). The modulus is the product of 719 and 919, so $\phi(660761) = 718 \cdot 918$, which is 502456. I send you the value $c = 120041$. When it comes time to decommit, I can send you as my secret the number 666 or the number $666 + 659124$ because these values have the same image under f.

One might think that one could remedy this problem by restricting the inputs of f to be less than $\phi(660761)$. This does not solve the problem because, as it turns out, $2^{54927} \equiv 1$ (mod 660761). Thus, for example, $f(666) = f(666 + 54927)$.

We see that one-way-ness is not sufficient to achieve commitment. In Chapter 14, we define *message digest functions*. We will see that a message digest function has exactly the property needed to implement commitment.

11.5. Problems

1. Consider the following table of modular exponentials:
   Mod 7 exponentiation (base 3)

x	3^x
0	1
1	3
2	2
3	6
4	4
5	5

   Such a table can be used to determine modular logarithms (also known as discrete logarithms). For a given number y, mod 7 $\log_3 y$ is the smallest nonnegative number x such that $3^x \equiv y$ (mod 7). For example, the mod 7 $\log_3$ of 6 is 3. (Just find 6 in the right column, and look to its left to find 3.)

   For this problem, construct a similar table for a modulus of 11 and a base of 3. Use it to determine the following modular logarithms.

(a) mod 11 $\log_3 6 =$?
(b) mod 11 $\log_3 2 =$?
(c) mod 11 $\log_3 4 =$?

2. The previous problem should suggest to you an algorithm for computing the logarithm of y mod m with base b, namely build an exponentiation table based on the values of m and b, and then look up y in the second column, and output the corresponding exponent x.

   (a) Explain using Euler's Theorem (Section 7.7) why the table need have no more than $m - 1$ rows.

   (b) How many multiplications are needed to construct such a table? Give a formula depending on m.

   (c) How many ticks are needed? Give a formula overestimating the number of ticks depending on m.

   (d) Recall the computer MegaComp described in Problem 14 of Section 10.5. Roughly how long would MegaComp take using this algorithm to calculate a modlog if the modulus is a 50-digit number?

3. There is a better algorithm known for computing a modlog than the one that builds a table. (It's too complicated to explain in this book.) The number of ticks required when the modulus is m is estimated by the following formula (where k is the number of digits in the modulus):

$$k^2 \cdot 10^{\sqrt{k \cdot (\log_{10} k)}}$$

   (a) How long would SlowThink take to compute a modlog using the better algorithm if the modulus m is a 50-digit number? Use a regular calculator to plug into the above formula.

   (b) Now MegaComp has been outfitted with the better algorithm for modlog. Our aim here is to explore its limits. How how many digits long would the modulus have to be in order for MegaComp to take more than a thousand years to calculate a modlog? (Try 50 digits, 60 digits, 70 digits ...)

4. In order to make a good choice of the security parameter, we must take into account the time required by algorithms required to *use* a scheme (e.g., encryption) and the time Eve requires to break it (e.g., decrypting without the key). When doing this sort of analysis, we will make the assumption that Eve is using the best possible algorithm and has access to the fastest computers available.

   For cryptographic schemes based on modular exponentiation, we use as the security parameter the number k of digits of the modulus. We have seen that the repeated squaring algorithm is a good algorithm for modular exponentiation: the number of ticks required is roughly $13 \cdot 2 \cdot k^3$. We also know that an algorithm exists for computing the inverse operation, modlog, one that requires roughly $k^2 \cdot 10^{\sqrt{(k)(log_{10}k)}}$ ticks.

Suppose that Alice's computer runs at 10^8 ticks per second. Although this is by no means slow, she must assume that Eve might possess a machine capable of running at the blinding speed of 10^{11} ticks per second. Assume Even uses the modlog algorithm mentioned above. Is there a value Alice can chose for the security parameter, k, which will allow her to encrypt a block of plaintext in about a second, while preventing Eve from decrypting it without spending volumes more time? Please give such a value for k and explain. Note: You can obtain the answer by using algebra, but in this case it is also perfectly acceptable to use a calculator and try different values of k.

5. Arnold has come up with a new proposal for a highly secure one-way function. The security parameter k is the number of digits of the modulus. We won't tell you precisely how the function is defined (it's classified), but we can tell you how long computations take (as a function of k). Let $A(x)$ denote the proposed one-way function.

> **Forward direction:** Given input x, to calculate $A(x)$ takes $2 \cdot k^6$ ticks.
> **Backward direction:** Given input y, to calculate a pre-image of y under A takes $10 \cdot k^{10}$ ticks.

What do you think of the proposed one-way function, based on what you know? Is it secure enough to recommend for use in financial transactions on the Internet?

6. Dopey, Sneezy, and Doc each propose a one-way function. For each of their schemes, the number of ticks for finding an image (going forward) and finding a pre-image (going backwards) are given in the table below as formulas depending on the security parameter n. Based on this table, which scheme is best, and why?

	No. of ticks to find image	No. of ticks to find pre-image
Dopey	n	n^2
Sneezy	n^2	2^n
Dox	$n - 100000$	$n + 100000$

12

Diffie and Hellman's Exponential-Key-Agreement Protocol

12.1. Motivation

One of the difficulties with traditional, symmetric-key cryptosystems is in getting the two parties to both know a secret key without anybody else knowing. This is particularly difficult when the two parties have never met in person and can only communicate via an insecure channel such as the Internet.

One could try to forestall the above difficulty by providing keys to everybody in advance. However, this introduces another difficulty. Suppose that there are a million and one people that want to participate. We can't know in advance who's going to want to communicate private with whom, so we have to provide each person a million keys, one for each of the other people with whom she might want to communicate. I couldn't possibly remember all these keys, so I have to store them on my computer. Suppose Eve has been eavesdropping on my communication and storing all the messages. If she manages to break into my computer and learn my keys, she can decrypt all these messages.

Worse yet, suppose another person comes along and wants to join the crowd. In order that the new person be able to communicate with everyone else, we have to provide a new key to each of the people already in the crowd. How can we transmit these new keys securely to all these people? (And who's this "we"? Who would you trust to securely generate and distribute secret keys?)

12.2. Background

Exponential key agreement[1] provides a way for you and me to agree on a key while communicating over an insecure channel. We can use this key only for one communication session, and then discard it. Because our computers don't

---

[1] Also called exponential key exchange.

143

retain the key, even if Eve later breaks into my computer, she can't decrypt our old communication traffic. There is no need to distribute millions of keys to all the people using the Internet, as any two people can agree on a key whenever they want.

The security of exponential key agreement depends in part on the modular logarithm problem being computationally difficult. As discussed in the previous chapter, if indeed this problem is difficult then modular exponentiation gives us a good way to "hide" a secret number x, that is, to calculate a number that *depends* on x but from which x cannot be easily computed. We calculate 2^x (mod m) using the repeated squaring method.

In this chapter, we use some other, special properties of exponentiation. In particular, we use the fact that raising a number X to the power Y and then raising the result to the power Z yields the same value as raising X to the power Z and raising that result to the power Y. In symbols,

$$(X^Y)^Z = X^{YZ} = (X^Z)^Y$$

and this is true even if the exponentiation uses modular arithmetic.

12.3. The protocol

Suppose Alice and Bob wish to select a secret key to facilitate their private communication over an insecure network. We assume the value of the modulus m is known to everyone in the network. Alice privately selects a large random number A, and calculates 2^A (mod m) using the repeated squaring algorithm. We will call the resulting number *AlicePart* because it is her contribution to the selection of the shared key. She sends *AlicePart* to Bob. Similarly, Bob privately selects a large random number B, and calculates 2^B (mod m), which we will call *BobPart*. He then sends *BobPart* to Alice.

Now the parties can calculate their shared key. Alice privately calculates her key by raising *BobPart* to the power of A, using modular arithmetic. Similarly, Bob calculates his key by raising *AlicePart* to the power of B, again using modular arithmetic. Because of the property of exponentiation described previously, the key Alice calculates and the key Bob calculates are the same number, as we now show:

$$
\begin{aligned}
\text{Alice's key} &= \textit{BobPart}^A \\
&= (2^B)^A \\
&= (2^A)^B \\
&= \textit{AlicePart}^B \\
&= \text{Bob's key}
\end{aligned}
$$

Thus the two parties now have a common key and can preserve their privacy while communicating over the insecure network, using, say, a traditional one-key cryptosystem.

12.4. Security

What does Eve learn from eavesdropping on the communication between Alice and Bob? She learns the number Alice is using as *AlicePart*, and she learns the number Bob is using as *BobPart*. In principle, therefore, she could determine the key. For example, she could calculate the base 2 mod m logarithm of *Alice-Part*, which is A. She could then, like Alice, calculate $BobPart^A$. The problem with this approach, of course, is that it would take Eve too long to calculate A (unless she knows of an exciting new algorithm for the modular logarithm problem) because the modulus is so big. She could similarly try to calculate Bob's secret number B, but this would probably be just as difficult.

Is there no other approach for Eve? Might there be another way for her to calculate the key from *AlicePart* and *BobPart*? Well, we don't know-there might be, but no better approach is known.

Does it make you nervous, the idea of relying for your privacy on some computational problems being difficult to solve? It might be that solving these problems is inherently too difficult, that nobody will discover a good algorithm for these problems because none exists. Certainly there are computational problems for which we can mathematically prove there is no good algorithm. However, there have also been breakthroughs in algorithms research, discoveries of algorithms that people thought didn't exist.

It seems inevitable that cryptography will rely on the uncertain. It has been said that cryptographers seldom sleep soundly. However, you should keep in mind an important but somewhat difficult point. For a traditional cryptographic system (such as a typical one-key encryption scheme), the security rests on the difficulty of a much more complicated and messy computational problem. You might think this would make such a problem less likely to be solvable, but in fact the messiness may be concealing what is fundamentally an easy problem. Paradoxically, the mathematical simplicity and clarity of the modular logarithm problem should give you more confidence, because if there were a fundamental weakness it would be more obvious. Then again, you never know.

12.5. Eve in the middle

There is one well-known attack Eve can mount on the exponential key agreement protocol. The attack does not depend on Eve being able to solve the modular logarithm problem. Instead, the attack depends on Eve being able to convince Alice and Bob they are communicating with each other, when they are actually communicating with Eve! Alice innocently sends her *AlicePart* across the network toward Bob. Eve intercepts this message. She calculates her own *EvePart* by choosing a number E and raising 2 to the power of E, and sends *EvePart* to Alice, pretending that she is Bob and that the number she sends is really *BobPart*. Alice calculates her key by raising *EvePart* to the power of A. Eve can calculate the same key by raising *AlicePart* to the power of E. Now when Alice sends a message through the network to Bob, encrypted with her key, Eve can intercept and decrypt the message.

In order to ensure that Alice and Bob do not detect the attack, Eve also carries out the same deception with Bob. Pretending to be Alice, Eve sends *EvePart* to Bob. Bob takes *EvePart* to be *AlicePart*, and sends his number *Bob-Part* to Alice. Eve intercepts this number. Now she knows the key Bob will use as well. Every time Alice sends a message to Bob, Eve intercepts it, decrypts it (using the key she shares with Alice), reads it, and re-encrypts it (using the key she shares with Bob), and then forwards it on to Bob. Similarly, every time Bob sends a message to Alice, Eve intercepts it, then decrypts and re-encrypts it using the appropriate keys. Thus Eve gets to see every message sent, and Alice and Bob never suspect a thing. (Eve can use the same approach to actually change the messages.)

This attack demonstrates the need for communicating parties to securely identify each other. There are ways to do this, but there are also many ways for the parties to *insecurely* identify each other, i.e. to use cryptographic techniques to convince themselves they are being secure when in fact they are not.

12.6. Problems

1. You are GuinEVEre. Alice and Bob are using base-2 exponential key agreement mod 83721983. Alice sent 78329101 as her part, and Bob sent 62974812 as his part. You eavesdropped on them.

   You want to know what key they have agreed upon. Fortunately, Merlin the Wizard is your buddy. He will calculate one (and only one) modular logarithm for you.

   (a) What modlog do you ask him to calculate for you? Be sure to give him all the necessary inputs.

   (b) Suppose his response is the number Z. Give a formula for Alice and Bob's key in terms of Z.

   (c) Merlin is on to you, and will refuse to answer any modlog questions involving numbers he sees Alice and Bob send to each other. Taking this into account, answer questions (a) and (b) again. (Solving this problem requires extreme cleverness.)

13

Computationally Secure Single-Key Cryptosystems

13.1. Secure block cyphers in the real world

We have seen that the addition cypher is not secure (unless used as a onetime pad). If you stick to one key and use the addition cypher as a block cypher, this cryptosystem is subject to a plaintext–cyphertext attack. Other attacks are effective as well.

There are lots of relatively secure cryptosystems, however. The most famous is DES (Data Encryption Standard). DES came out of an effort in 1970 by the National Bureau of Standards (NBS) to select a standard cryptosystem for use with non-classified data. In 1974, in response to the NBS's public appeal for a cryptosystem, IBM submitted a cryptosystem called Lucifer that they had developed earlier that decade. NBS then went to the National Security Agency (NSA) for help in evaluating the cryptosystem. NSA modified the system somewhat, including a reduction of the key size from the 112 bits used by Lucifer to only 56 bits (a compromise, as NSA had tried to reduce it to 48 bits). The resulting system was then certified by NBS for use. Institutions that needed to communicate privately with the government were expected to use DES (unless the material was classified). In 1979 the American Bankers Association recommended use of DES for encryption. Thus DES achieved very broad use.

At this point, the technology is such that 56-bit keys do not make for a large enough key space. Keep in mind that DES is used for banking transactions. The number of possible keys is roughly 10^{17}. In 1997, in response to a challenge, a team called DESCHALL found a DES key by brute-force search 96 days after the announcement of the challenge. The search was carried out using thousands of computers made available via the Internet by their owners. A similar challenge was solved in 41 days in early 1998. The Electronic Frontier Foundation, a nonprofit organization, spent under $250,000 to build a special-purpose

147

machine, Deep Crack, that was able to find a DES key in 56 hours. In 2005, the National Institute of Standards and Technology (NIST), the successor to NBS, withdrew DES as a standard.

There are variants of DES that are more secure. A system called Triple DES involves three encryptions of the cleartext, one after the other, using different keys. (For reasons we won't go into, double DES is not much more secure than ordinary DES.) Triple DES is sometimes used with only two keys, one for the first and third encryption, and one for the middle encryption. When DES is used this way, the number of bits of key is 112. NIST has approved Triple DES for use through 2030.

Since the invention of DES, other cryptosystems have been invented by individuals not associated with the government. IDEA (International Data Encryption Algorithm) uses 128 bits of key and was invented by Lai and Massey. Some systems have been proposed but then shown to be insecure. A cryptosystem called Skipjack has been designed by the NSA for use in chips manufactured by government-authorized manufacturers. The design of Skipjack was initially classified. Thus the design of Skipjack was not made available for cryptanalysts to try cracking it. For this reason, some people had less confidence in the security of Skipjack. It was declassified in 1998.

In 2001, NIST selected an new encryption standard, designated the Advanced Encryption Standard (AES). It allows for key sizes of 128, 192, and 256 bits.

13.2. Cypher block chaining

In Chapter 3, Section 3.2, we discussed the idea of a block cypher: starting with a cryptosystem for encrypting blocks of a limited size, one can build a cryptosystem that can encrypt messages of arbitrary length. We outlined one such method, called ECB mode. We discussed the insecurity of ECB mode in Section 3.4. In this section, we outline a somewhat more secure method of building a block cypher, called *cypher block chaining*, abbreviated CBC.

The problem with ECB was that each block of plaintext was encrypted independently of every other. CBC is perhaps the simplest thing one can imagine to eliminate that independence. It is represented in Figure 13.1. The first block of cyphertext depends only on the first block of plaintext. The second block of cyphertext depends only on the second block of plaintext *and* the first block of cyphertext (and thus indirectly on the first block of plaintext). The third block of cyphertext depends only on the third block of plaintext and on the second block of cyphertext (and thus indirectly on the first and second blocks of plaintext). And so on. The same key is used for each block encryption.

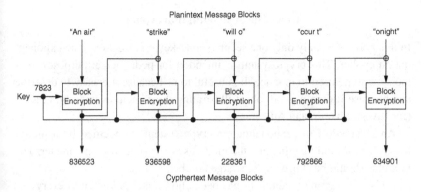

Figure 13.1. A diagram of cypher block chaining.

In particular, to get the second block of cyphertext, one first combines the second block of plaintext with the first block of cyphertext in some way. For our purposes, modular addition suffices: the two are added together modulo m, where m is $10^{number\ of\ digits\ in\ a\ block}$. One then encrypts the sum using the block encryption method.[1] One similarly obtained the third block of cyphertext by adding together the second block of cyphertext, and then encrypting the result. And so on.

This method is not as secure as one might hope. If the first few blocks of two messages coincide, the corresponding cyphertexts will coincide as well. For this reason, a slight change is made to this basic scheme: a random number called the *initialization vector* (and abbreviated IV) is combined with the first block of plaintext before it gets encrypted. Thus the IV plays the role of the zeroth block of cyphertext in cypher block chaining. The intended recipient of the message would not be able to decrypt the message without knowing the IV, so the IV is transmitted (in the clear, i.e., unencrypted) along with the encrypted message.

When IVs are used, even if two plaintexts start out the same, the corresponding cyphertexts will probably differ from the start because the IVs chosen for the different encryptions will most probably be different. In fact, even if the plaintexts are completely identical, the cyphertexts will be different. Use of randomness has helped us to make the system more secure.

---

[1] In real systems, the combining is slightly different. Each block is written in base 2 (binary, the number system used by digital computers). Each pair of corresponding binary digits in the two blocks are then combined by addition mod 2 to get a new binary digit. The sequence of binary digits thus obtained is taken to be the representation of the combined number, and is encrypted using block encryption. This combining method is easier for computers than the system we use.

13.3. The exponentiation cypher

In this book, we study only one secure single-key cryptosystem, the exponentiation cypher. This cryptosystem is intended for pedagogical purposes. It is too slow to be used in practice. It is useful to us because it is easy to describe and because it does a good job of illustrating the principles underlying RSA (for Rivest, Shamir, and Adleman).

An instance of the exponentiation cryptosystem is specified by a modulus m. You should imagine that the modulus is a system-wide parameter. The modulus should be chosen to be a large number.

Let's say a prime modulus m has been chosen and is known to everyone. The encryption function is

$$encrypt(plain, key) = plain^{key} \pmod{m}$$

Here the value of *plain* should be a positive integer that is less than the modulus m. As always, the intention is that the key is chosen randomly. In this case, the key should be a positive number less than $m - 1$. If the key is a very small integer (e.g., 1), the encryption will not be secure, but if the modulus is huge (as it should be), a randomly chosen key is extremely unlikely to be small.

In fact, for reasons that will be apparent when we discuss decryption, not all positive numbers less than $m - 1$ are acceptable as keys. However, enough of them are that this should not be a problem.

Before we go into decryption, consider whether the system is susceptible to a plaintext–cyphertext attack, in which Eve knows a block of plaintext and the corresponding block of cyphertext. Finding the key from this information amounts to solving the equation

$$b^x \equiv c \pmod{m}$$

for x, where b is the plaintext and c is the cyphertext. This is the modular-logarithm problem, which we think is computationally difficult. Thus there is reason to believe that the exponentiation cypher is secure against a plaintext-cyphertext attack. Even if Eve learns many plaintext–cyphertext pairs, it probably won't help her.

Now we consider decryption. This uses number theory discussed in a previous chapter. Let s be the $mod\phi(m)$ multiplicative inverse of *key*. Then the way to decrypt a cyphertext *cyph* is to raise it to the power of s mod m. That is,

$$plain = cyph^s \pmod{m}$$

Does this work? If so, why? The answer lies partly in what it means for s to be the mod$\phi(m)$ multiplicative inverse of *key*. The definition of multiplicative inverse says that

$$key \cdot s \equiv 1 \pmod{\phi(m)}$$

This means that *key* multiplied by s minus something times $\phi(m)$ equals 1. Let d be the something. We then write

$$key \cdot s \equiv 1 + d \cdot \phi(m)$$

Now we use Euler's Theorem to show that the decryption method (usually) works. Euler's Theorem, which is discussed in the chapter on number theory, is reproduced below.

Euler's Theorem: For any modulus m, for any number b that is relatively prime to m,

$$b^{\phi(m)} \equiv 1 \pmod{m}$$

We want to show that if the plaintext is first raised to the power of *ley* (mod m) and then the result is raised to the power of s (mod m), the final result will be the plaintext.

$$\begin{aligned}
(plain^{key})^s &= plain^{key \cdot s} \text{ by a rule of exponentiation} \\
&= plain^{1 + d \cdot \phi(m)} \text{ by substitution} \\
&= plain^1 plain^{d \cdot \phi(m)} \text{ by the adding-exponents rule of} \\
&\quad \text{exponentiation} \\
&= plain^1 (plain^{\phi(m)})^d \text{ by the multiplying-exponents rule of} \\
&\quad \text{exponentiation}
\end{aligned}$$

Now by Euler's Theorem, since *clear* is relatively prime to m (every positive integer less than m is relatively prime to m since m is prime), we have

$$plain^{\phi(m)} \equiv 1 \pmod{m}$$

We therefore have that

$$plain^1 (plain^{\phi(m)})^d \equiv plain^1 (1)^d \pmod{m}$$

and of course $plain^1 1^d$ is the plaintext, *plain*. Therefore $cyph^s$ rem m is the plaintext.

Now we know that decryption works. Is it doable? Can someone who knows the key carry out the decryption. They would need to calculate mod $\phi(m)$, but that's easy: because m is a prime, $\phi(m) = m - 1$. Then they would need to calculate the mod $\phi(m)$ multiplicative inverse of the key. Now a problem arises: the key only has such a multiplicative inverse if it is relatively prime to $\phi(m)$. If it is, then Euclid's algorithm can be used to find the inverse. Thus when a number is chosen to be used as the key, Euclid's algorithm should be used to try to find the mod $\phi(m)$ multiplicative inverse. If Euclid's algorithm fails, a different number should be randomly chosen to serve as the key. Because most numbers are relatively prime to $\phi(m)$, it should take only a few attempts before a number is chosen that does have an inverse.

Once the multiplicative inverse s has been determined, decryption consists of just raising the cyphertext to the power of s (mod m). This can be done quickly using the repeated squaring algorithm.

13.4. How to find a big prime

The exponentiation cypher requires that the modulus be a huge prime number. Huge prime numbers are also used in RSA (to be discussed in other chapters). How can one get a huge prime? The answer to this question has two parts.

The first part of the answer is a fast way of testing if a number is prime. Before Euler proved his theorem, Fermat (a lawyer and bureaucrat who "dabbled" in mathematics, producing extremely important and influential mathematical ideas) proved a special case of it, the case where the modulus m is prime. In this case, $\phi(m) = m - 1$. Thus Fermat's Theorem says that for every prime m, for any b relatively prime to m,

$$b^{m-1} \equiv 1 \quad (\text{mod } m) \tag{13.1}$$

Is this true for moduli m that are not prime? Some special composite (non-prime) numbers, called Carmichael numbers, behave like primes in this respect: if m is a Carmichael number then Eq. (13.1) holds true for every b relatively prime to m. However, Carmichael numbers are fairly rare. For most composite numbers m, Eq. (13.1) is false for at least half the b's.

This gives a way to test a number m to see if it is composite. Choose a random b, and use the repeated-squaring algorithm to see if Eq. (13.1) is true. If not, you have shown that m is not prime (if m were prime, the equation would hold regardless of the choice of b). If the equation turns out to be true, choose another random b and try again. Run through this procedure 30 times or so, choosing a random b each time. If in every trial you find that the equation is true, you can pretty safely conclude that m is either a prime number or a Carmichael number.

How do we determine if m is a Carmichael number or a prime? There is a very similar but somewhat more sophisticated test that can do that.

This test gives us a way of obtaining a 100-digit prime. Namely, choose a random 100-digit number, and test it to see if it is prime. If not, choose another random 100-digit number and try again. Keep going until you choose a number that turns out to be prime.

How many numbers are you likely to try? The answer to that question hinges on the rarity of primes. If primes are extremely rare, you will probably have to try lots of numbers before coming upon a prime. If primes are plentiful, it won't take you long.

Fortunately, primes are somewhat plentiful. An important theorem in number theory called (duh) the Prime Number Theorem states essentially that among k-digit numbers, roughly one out of $2.3k$ are prime. This estimate is only a good estimate when k is pretty big, say bigger than 50. For $k = 100$, this says that roughly one out of 230 numbers is prime. Consequently, the average number of tries before you come across a number that happens to be prime is 230. That's only the average – you might have to do more tries in a particular case-but you're not likely to need more than, say 2300 tries. Fast enough if you have a good computer.

13.5. Problems

For the first three problems, you will consider different exponentiation cyphers corresponding to different moduli. For each, you will consider several different keys. Remember that for a modulus m and key k, the encryption function is

$$f(clear) = clear^k \pmod{m}$$

Remember also that the rule for the decryption function has the form

$$g(cyph) = cyph^s \pmod{m}$$

1. For the following values of *modulus* and *key*, give the decrypting exponent s (i.e., the number to which the cyphertext should be raised to get the plaintext). If no such exponent exists, explain why.

   You might find the following tables of modular inverses useful. We write the multiplicative inverse of a number x as x^{-1}.
   (a) *key* = 5 and *modulus* = 17
   (b) *key* = 15 and *modulus* = 17
   (c) *key* = 2 and *modulus* = 19
   (d) *key* = 12 and *modulus* = 19
   (e) *key* = 0 and *modulus* = 23
   (f) *key* = 13 and *modulus* = 23
   In the first two problems, you will use Euclid's algorithm to find the value of s (the mod-$\phi(m)$ multiplicative inverse of k).

x	x^{-1} (mod 16)	x	x^{-1} (mod 18)	x	x^{-1} (mod 22)
0	–	0	–	0	–
1	1	1	1	1	1
2	–	2	–	2	–
3	11	3	–	3	15
4	–	4	–	4	–
5	13	5	11	5	9
6	–	6	–	6	–
7	7	7	13	7	19
8	–	8	–	8	–
9	9	9	–	9	5
10	–	10	–	10	–
11	3	11	5	11	–
12	–	12	–	12	–
13	5	13	7	13	17
14	–	14	–	14	–
15	15	15	–	15	3
		16	–	16	–
		17	17	17	13
				18	–
				19	7
				20	–
				21	21

For part A, *determine the value of s using EuclidCards. Please make copies and cut out and tape together the cards as appropriate. If the given key k does not have a mod-ϕ(m) multiplicative inverse, you should say so, and specify an integer greater than 1 that divides both k and ϕ(m).*

For part B, *if you successfully found an s in part A, demonstrate by algebra and arithmetic and Euler's Theorem that the decryption function you found does indeed reverse the action of the encryption function.*

Example: Modulus $m = 1091$, key $k = 533$

Part a:

Part b:

Let c denote the plaintext.

$$
\begin{aligned}
(c^{533})^{227} &= c^{120991} \\
&= c^{1090 \cdot 111 + 1} \\
&= (c^{1090})^{111})c^1 \\
&\equiv (1)^{111}c^1 \pmod{1091} \\
&= c
\end{aligned}
$$

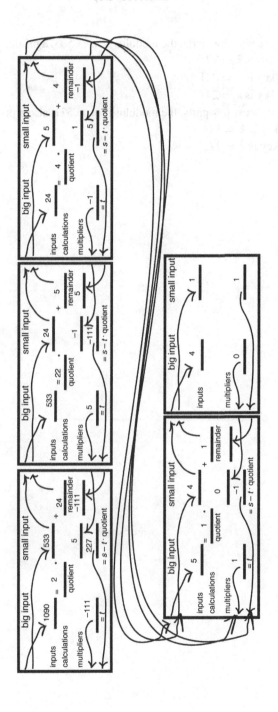

(a) For the next few parts, the modulus is $m = 503$, a prime.
    i. key is $k = 37$
    ii. key is $k = 241$
    iii. key is $k = 24$
(b) For the next few parts, the modulus is $m = 571$, also a prime.
    i. key is $k = 133$
    ii. key is $k = 77$

14

Public-Key Cryptosystems and
Digital Signatures

14.1. Public-key cryptosystems

The key agreement protocol provides a way for previously unacquainted parties to agree on a secret key. However, there are times when one party wants to unilaterally send a private message to another party without first interacting with the other party. Public-key encryption, first proposed by Diffie and Hellman in the early 1970s, provides a way to accomplish this.

In traditional (one-key) cryptography, the same key is used to encrypt a message as to decrypt it. Public-key cryptography discards this convention, and allows one (public) key to be used for encryption and another (the secret key) for decryption.

The set-up for public key cryptography is as follows. Every person intending to receive encrypted messages privately chooses a secret key and calculates a corresponding public key. All the public keys are made publically available. If I want to send an encrypted message to someone, I look up her public key and use it to encrypt a message to her; only she is able to decrypt it.

The idea of having different keys for encryption and decryption seems simple, but it represented a startling break with the past. It is worth considering why the discovery was so late in coming; after all, traditional cryptography has been used for a few thousand years. Why did the idea of two different keys not arise earlier?

Note that the secret key and the public key must be closely related for the decryption to work. In principle, they have the same information content. Thus it seems as if knowing one-say, the public key-would be tantamount to knowing the other. (Analogously, if you know a function, encryption, then one would think you would also know its inverse, decryption.) Thus there would be no point in having two different keys – they would only be two different ways of representing the same information.

This argument, while persuasive, is flawed, for it fails to take into account computational limitations. It is true that knowing the public key in principle enables one to calculate the secret key; however, that calculation might require so much time, even on the fastest computer, as to be impossible in a practical sense. I suspect, however, that the flawed argument was in part the reason public-key cryptography was not proposed earlier. Detecting the flaw – or even realizing that such an argument was nontrivial – required a degree of sophistication about computational processes that people lacked before the development of computers and of theoretical computer science.

14.2. El Gamal's cryptosystem

Enough advertising; now we describe a public-key cryptosystem. The system we describe is a slight variant of one proposed by Tahir El Gamal. This was not the first such cryptosystem proposed – the RSA (Rivest, Shamir, abd Adleman) cryptosystem was first – but it is easy to understand once you have understood exponential key agreement, which we now review.

Let m be a system-wide modulus. In the key agreement protocol, Alice chooses a secret random number A, and sends 2^A (mod m) to Bob. Bob similarly chooses a secret random number B, and sends 2^B (mod m) to Alice. Then they are both able to calculate a key 2^{AB} (mod m). Alice calculates this key by taking the number sent to her by Bob, 2^B, and raising it to the power of A. Bob calculates the same key by taking the number sent to him by Alice, 2^A, and raising it to the power of B.

The essential idea of El Gamal's scheme is to take a piece of the key agreement protocol and make it instead part of the set-up. In particular, during the set-up Bob chooses a number *BobSecret* to be used as his secret key. He calculates $2^{BobSecret}$ (mod m) and publicizes this number, which we shall call *BobPublic*. Now when Alice wants to send an encrypted message to Bob, she first looks up Bob's public key, and finds that it is the number *BobPublic*. Next she essentially follows the key agreement protocol but instead of waiting for Bob to send his *BobPart*, she uses *BobPublic* as *BobPart*. That is, Alice chooses a random number A, then calculates *AlicePart* $= 2^A$ (mod m). Then she calculates the key by raising *BobPublic* to the power A (in modular arithmetic). She encrypts her plaintext using that key in the manner of a one-time pad, by adding the plaintext to the key modulo m. Finally, she sends Bob a two-part message. The first part is *AlicePart*, and the second part is the cyphertext.

Bob can determine the key, essentially as he does in the exponential key agreement protocol, by raising *AlicePart* to the power of *BobSecret*. He then uses this key to decrypt the cyphertext, obtaining the plaintext.

The above description may be confusing because there are so many numbers that might be described as keys. There is *BobSecret*, which is Bob's secret key. There is *BobPublic*, which is Bob's public key. All well and good; we knew that public-key cryptography involved two keys, one public and one secret. But there is also the key finally used by Alice to encrypt her plaintext; the same key is used by Bob to decrypt. What is this third key doing in our cryptosystem? It is sort of a "disposable" key, used just once to encrypt just one message. While essential to the functioning of the El Gamal cryptosystem, it does not appear in other public-key cryptosystems and does not play a role in the concept of a public-key cryptosystem.

Think of public-key cryptosystems as automobiles. There is essentially one way to drive an automobile, regardless of whether it runs on gasoline or on electricity. In a gas-driven auto, the carburetor is an essential part, but it has nothing to do with the concept of an auto. Similarly, every public-key cryptosystem has a public key and a secret key, and from a high-level view these are used in the same way in every public-key cryptosystem, but the details differ. The disposable key is in this sense like the carburetor.

The most famous (and the first) public-key cryptosystem proposed, the RSA cryptosystem, doesn't involve a disposable key. Indeed, RSA is conceptually simpler than El Gamal, but is based on slightly more sophisticated mathematics. We will describe the RSA cryptosystem shortly.

It is interesting that Diffie and Hellman, who discovered both exponential key agreement and the concept of a public-key cryptosystem, failed to discover the El Gamal system, which is so similar to key agreement. The reason may be that Diffie and Hellman thought about public-key cryptography in terms of a mathematical notion called a *trapdoor one-way function*, and were looking for a cryptosystem that was based on that notion. El Gamal's system is not based on that idea. For this reason, perhaps, it was not in Diffie and Hellman's line of sight. We explain the notion of a trapdoor one-way function soon.

14.3. More remarks about the El Gamal cryptosystem

Now I return to the specifics of the El Gamal cryptosystem, and make some technical remarks. It is important that a new third key be selected every time a new message is sent. (We know from the VENONA story the danger of reusing a one-time pad!) Therefore, Alice must select a new number A each time she wants to encrypt a message. What about when someone else (Bob, for example) wants to send a message to Alice? For such occasions, Alice has her own secret key AliceSecret and her own public key *AlicePublic*. Bob chooses a number B (just to be used for encrypting one message) and so on, using *AlicePublic* as *AlicePart*. The point is that the number A that Alice selects when she wants to encrypt a message has nothing to do with the number *AliceSecret* she uses to decrypt a message sent to her.

Note that because the third key is chosen anew each time by a random process, two encryptions of the same plaintext are very likely to be different. That is, unlike all other cryptosystems we have studied, for this system the cyphertext depends not only on the plaintext and the key but also on some random stuff. This might sound like a disadvantage ("the cyphertext is unpredictable!") but it is usually an advantage: an eavesdropper who intercepts multiple cyphertexts cannot tell which of them correspond to identical plaintexts. There is a disadvantage: the cyphertext is at least twice as long as the plaintext – it consists of two numbers, each having at least as many digits as the plaintext – because it depends on more than just the plaintext.

14.4. Public-key cryptography in practice

What does one do when the document to be encrypted consists of many more digits than the modulus? Note that this sort of problem can arise with any cryptosystem, public-key or traditional. The standard solution is to use the system as a block cypher: break the document into smaller *blocks*, and encrypt each block separately.

For practical purposes, however, there is an obstacle to the use of publickey cryptosystems (El Gamal or RSA) in encrypting huge documents. The modulus must be quite big (a couple of hundred digits at least) in order for the system be secure; otherwise, an eavesdropper with reasonable computing resources could crack the system. However, with such a big modulus, exponentiating takes a while, even using a fast algorithm such as repeated squaring. This is not an issue if the document is short (a few thousand digits), but if the document consists of millions of digits, it is a big issue.

The advantages of public-key cryptography are too great to give up entirely, however. The solution? Use public-key cryptography to encrypt a 100-digit number k, and send that encryption. Then use k as the key to encrypt the document using a fast, one-key system such as DES, and send that encryption. The recipient first determines the key k using his knowledge of his secret key, then use k as a key with DES to decrypt the big document.

14.5. Signatures

In the physical world of paper and pens, I typically sign a document to indicate that I approve of it. Anyone who later sees the signed document is convinced of my approval of it. For example, if the document is a contract, my signature is physical evidence of my promise to uphold the contract. Furthermore, it is considered somewhat difficult to forge a signature; it is hard for someone other than me to create a signature that looks like mine.

In the digital world, where copying pieces of one document into another is a simple matter, the notion of signing a document is subtler. In the physical world, I try to make all my signatures look the same, for if my signature varies a lot, a forged signature is more likely to be accepted as mine. In the digital world, my signature should not simply consist of a specific unvarying piece of data appended to a document, else an eavesdropper who sees one legitimately signed document could copy that piece of data to other documents, effectively forging my signature.

Instead, my digital signature for a document depends mathematically on the content of the document. You can verify that my purported signature on a document really comes from me by examining the document and the signature, and verifying that the mathematical relationship holds between them. In order, therefore, that anyone be able to verify a signature is indeed mine, the required mathematical relationship should be publically known. At the same time, in order that only I be able to produce signatures construed as mine, the mathematical relationship should be closely related to some secret that only I possess.

At this point you should be reminded of the concept of public-key cryptography, in which anyone can encrypt a message intended for me, but only I can decrypt it. Both public-key cryptography and digital signatures depend on there being a public datum and a secret datum for each person. The secret datum for a person is a number that only that person knows; knowing this secret enables the person to accomplish some task, such as decrypting or creating a signature. The public datum for a person is a number that is publically linked to the person; given the person's name, anyone can determine the corresponding public datum, and use it to encrypt a message for that person or verify that person's signature.

The close similarity between public-key cryptography and digital signatures is no accident; both ideas were discovered by Diffie and Hellman and described in a paper they wrote in the 1970s. Indeed, they described an abstract mathematical construction, called a *trapdoor one-way function*, that can serve as the basis for both public-key cryptography and digital signatures.

14.6. Trapdoor one-way functions and their use in public-key encryption and digital signatures

We have seen the idea of a *one-way function*; it is a function for which going forward (given an input, compute the corresponding output) is easy but going backward (given an output, compute the corresponding input) is computationally difficult. Diffie and Hellman took that concept and modified it in a small but significant way. A one-way function has a *trapdoor* if there is a piece of information, a secret, such that knowing the secret makes it easy to go backward. The secret is the trapdoor.

Let us see how a trapdoor one-way function can be used in public-key cryptography. To enable people to send encrypted messages to me, I construct and publish a description of a trapdoor one-way function for which I know the trapdoor. The function is used for encryption. Because the function is publically known, anyone can encrypt a message for me; the input to the function is the plaintext, and the output is the cyphertext. Decryption consists in applying the inverse of the function, that is, from the output of the function (the cyphertex), one must calculate the input (the plaintext). This calculation is difficult for someone who does not know the trapdoor. Because I know the trapdoor, I can do the calculation.

Next let us see how a trapdoor one-way function can be used in digital signatures. Again I construct and publish a description of a trapdoor oneway function for which I know the trapdoor. To obtain the signature for a document, I determine which input to the function would produce the document as output. I can do this calculation because I know the trapdoor. Now anyone who sees the signature can apply the function to it, obtaining an output. The output exactly matches the document if the signature is legitimate. Nobody but me can produce signature for a given document, because nobody but me possesses the secret, the trapdoor, that makes it easy to apply the inverse of the function.

In this chapter, I describe one function that, as far as we know, is a trapdoor one-way function. That is, it is believed that there is no good algorithm for going backwards, applying the inverse of the function, without knowing the trapdoor, but this belief has not been proven correct. This function was first proposed by Rivest, Shamir, and Adleman for use in public-key cryptography and in digital signatures; for this reason, the public-key cryptosystem is called the RSA cryptosystem, and the digital signature scheme is called the RSA signature scheme.

Note that the above method of using a trapdoor one-way function for public-key cryptography and for digital signatures is not the only way to achieve these purposes. In fact, the El Gamal public-key cryptosystem is not based on a trapdoor one-way function. El Gamal also proposed a digital signature scheme that is not based on such a function.

14.7. The RSA trapdoor one-way function

Here's how to create a trapdoor one-way function. Secretly choose two large (hundred-digit) prime numbers p and q such that $p - 1$ and $q - 1$ are not divisible by 3. Secretly multiply p and q, obtaining a number m. Now publicize the number m; it is your public key. The one-way function is modulo m cubing: $x \rightarrow x^3$ (mod m). It is easy for anyone who knows your public key m to calculate the output for any input. However, going the other way is believed to be difficult for anyone who doesn't know m's prime factors p and q.

You know these numbers because you selected them, so you can go the other way. Calculate $\Phi(m)$ by multiplying $p - 1$ and $q - 1$, and then calculate the mod $\Phi(m)$ multiplicative inverse s of 3. Finally, to calculate the modulo m cube root of a number, raise that number to the power of s (modulo m).

In fact, RSA does not tell you to use the number 3; you can use another number instead. For example, you could use the number 5 as long as $p - 1$ and $q - 1$ are not divisible by 5. There are some weaknesses associated with use of a small exponent, but they can be overcome using random encryption (discussed in the chapter on secure single-key encryption).

14.8. The RSA public-key cryptosystem

We can use this function in a cryptosystem. If your friend Alice wants to send you a message that only you can read, she encrypts her message by cubing it and then sending you the primary name (modulo m) of the cube. You can decrypt this by raising it to the power of s (modulo m).

14.9. The RSA digital signature scheme

We can also use the function in a digital signature scheme. Say the number b represents a document for which you want to construct a signature. You calculate the modulo m cube root of b by raising b to the power of s (modulo m). The result is your signature. You can send the document and the signature to anyone-if the recipient knows your public key m, she can verify that the signature matches the document. Namely, she cubes the signature (modulo m) and checks that it equals the document.

As for security, we believe (i.e., we hope) that an eavesdropper Eve can't forge a signature; i.e., for a document of her choosing determine the modulo m cube root of the document. Even if Eve sees a document and a signature created by you, we believe she can't calculate a signature for a slightly modified version of the document.

14.10. Message digest functions

There are many, many applications of digital signatures. Digital signatures are probably more important in practice than encryption. For example, a software company might send their new Web browsing software to users over the Internet. There is a danger that some hacker might modify the software en route to the users, introducing security holes. To enable the users to check that they have received a legitimate, unmodified copy of the software, the software company treats the new software as a document, and calculates and publicizes their signature for it. When a user receives her copy, she cubes the signature (modulo the public key of the software company) and checks that it matches the software.

However, as with public-key cryptography, there is a practical difficulty. For a huge document (e.g., software), the modulus would have to be huge as well, and consequently calculating the signature would take too long.

There is a security difficulty with RSA signatures as well. Even without knowing the secret key corresponding to a given public modulus, it is possible to construct [document,signature] pairs that would be accepted as valid for that public modulus. The catch is that the documents created this way are not meaningful. Still, this can be a security flaw in some applications.

The solution involves the use of a *cryptographic hash function* or a *message digest function*. This is a function that takes a very long document as its input and produces as output a small (40- or 50-digit) number. Small changes in the input result in large changes in the output. Furthermore, for a given output of the function, it is supposed to be difficult to find any input that gives rise to that output. In this way, a cryptographic hash function is very similar to a one-way function. The difference is that a cryptographic hash function is not one-to-one, so it does not have an inverse. However, the basic idea – "easy to go forward, hard to go backward" – is the same. More importantly, a cryptographic hash function has an additional security requirement, one of the following:

weakly collision-free: Given a document d, it should be computationally difficult to calculate a different document d^1 such that the image of d under the hash function equals the image of d^1.
strongly collision-free: It should be computationally difficult to calculate two different documents $d_1 d_2$ whose images under the hash function are equal.

The second condition implies the first and is in fact somewhat stronger. For some applications, the stronger condition is needed. For signature applications, the weaker condition should be enough.

To construct the signature for a long document, use the document as input to a publically known cryptographic hash function. The output is a small number. Then use the RSA signature scheme to calculate the signature for that small number. This can be calculated quickly because the modulus need only be a couple of hundred digits. Send the document and this signature. The recipient can check the validity of the signature and document as follows. She first uses the document as the input to the cryptographic hash function (the same one you used). Then she cubes the signature (modulo your public key) and checks that it matches the output of the cryptographic hash function.

If the cryptographic hash function is weakly collision-free, a hacker cannot modify the document en route without the modification being detected; the signature will be invalid for the modified document.

There are cryptographic hash functions that can produce an output very quickly, even if the input is a big document. It is believed (hoped) that these are secure ("hard to go backward"). However, some of these schemes (such as MD4 and MD5) have been shown to be insecure. *Caveat emptor*!

14.11. Use of message digest functions in commitment

Recall that in Chapter 11, we proposed using one-way functions to achieve commitment. We showed use of a nonce ensured that the commitment was not revealed until the proper time. However, we saw that use of a one-way function did not ensure that the commitment was binding.

Message digest functions provide a solution to this problem. If the oneway function is also strongly collision-free (i.e., the function is a message digest function) then the commitment is binding. Let f be a message digest function that is strongly collision-free. Suppose I wanted to commit to one value, say d_1, by sending you $f(d_1)$, and then possibly change my mind later and claim that d_2 was my original value. For you to believe me, d_1 and d_2 must have the same image under f, that is, $f(d_1) = f(d_2)$. Because f is strongly collision-free, I can't even come up with such a pair of values d_1 and d_2. Thus I am prevented from cheating.

14.12. Problems

1. Bilbo proposes the following function be used as a message digest function for signing arbitrarily long documents. The function is $f(x) = 2x$ rem m,

where m is a 100-digit prime number. Bilbo suggests you represent your document as a huge number (possibly consisting of thousands of digits), then calculate the image of that number under f. The resulting message digest is a mod-m standard name.

Now, we know that Bilbo's function is not an ideal message digest function because for a long document it might take minutes or even hours to find the image. If it were a secure message digest function, however, we might be willing to wait that long. Unfortunately, it is highly insecure.

(a) Describe the security goal for a message digest function, and explain what bad thing(s) could happen if an insecure message digest function were used with a digital signature scheme, and why the insecurity of the MD function makes the bad thing(s) possible.

(b) Show that Bilbo's function fails to achieve the security goal, and that if it were used in a signature scheme, Eve could exploit this flaw to modify a signed document without her modifications being detected. *Hint*: Recall Euler's Theorem.

2. You saw Boris Badinov encrypting a message, and managed to read only the first few blocks of plaintext: "Dear Natasha: I've recruited a new spy in the CIA. His name is"

You rush to your interception equipment, and manage to eavesdrop on all the blocks of cyphertext. You now turn to your collection of supercomputers...

In each of the following scenarios, **briefly describe how you would go about trying to determine the rest of the plaintext from the cyphertext. Be specific. Also, for each scenario, choose (i), (ii), or (iii) from the following:** are you (i) likely to succeed, (ii) unlikely to succeed within a year, (iii) simply not going to succeed no matter how long you live?

(a) Each block is encrypted by mod-1000000000000 addition of a key k. The same key is used for all the blocks.
- *attack?*
- *success likelihood?*

(b) As above, each block is encrypted using mod-1000000000000 addition, but now a different key is chosen for each block.
- *attack?*
- *success likelihood?*

(c) Each block is encrypted using the exponentiation cypher with a prime modulus of 251003. The same key is used for all the blocks.
- *attack?*
- *success likelihood?*

(d) Each block is encrypted using Natasha's RSA public modulus of 6355170039495021706507715343468563768585225538618713549420 9917... 6495012237225563812839425115194276145439 and a public exponent of 3.
  • *attack?*
  • *success likelihood?*

3. The naive way to use RSA encryption is to directly encrypt the plaintext using RSA, that is, raise the plaintext to the power of the recipient's public exponent (often 3) modulo the recipient's public modulus. As mentioned in Section 14.4, a better way is to choose a big random key K, encrypt K directly using RSA, and send the encryption of K, then encrypt the real plaintext using a single-key cryptosystem like DES or RC4, and send the resulting cyphertext.

Consider the following proposal: whenever a new user needs an account, she selects her password, encrypts it using the public key of the system administrator, and sends the cyphertext to the system administrator via email.

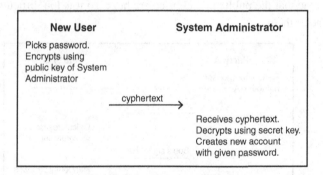

(a) **Show that if naive RSA encryption is used, Eve can benefit from a dictionary attack.**
(b) **Why does the better RSA encryption method render the dictionary attack impossible?**

4. Just as we previously used a challenge-response protocol based on ordinary, symmetric-key cryptography (in IFF, Identification Friend or Foe), we can use a challenge-response protocol based on public-key cryptography, RSA in particular. The goal is to make it possible for a party to know who she's communicating with. Suppose Carole is communicating with someone who claims to be Dave. Carole knows Dave's public key (she has previously obtained a certificate for Dave). Carole sends a random challenge R to the

other party, who responds by sending back Dave's signature for the value R. Carole can use Dave's public key to check that the signature for R is valid; because only Dave possesses the secret key that would enable someone to sign as Dave, Carole is convinced that she is talking to Dave.

Carole chooses R according to the uniform distribution on mod-m numbers, where m is Dave's public modulus. We assume m is a huge number (too big to factor), so there are so many possibilities for R that it is extremely unlikely Dave has ever previously calculated the signature for the particular R chosen. It is also extremely unlikely that R is a number (e.g., 1) for which anyone can compute the signature without knowing the secret key.

Consider the following protocol to enable two parties to mutually identify each other. Party A is claiming to be Alice, and party B is claiming to be Bob.

(a) Party A chooses a random challenge R_A and sends it to Party B.
(b) Party B responds by sending Bob's signature for the value R_A, and by sending a random challenge R_B of his own.
(c) Party A responds by sending Alice's signature for the value R_B.

Assume that the public moduli used are huge, so it is too difficult for Eve to factor them.

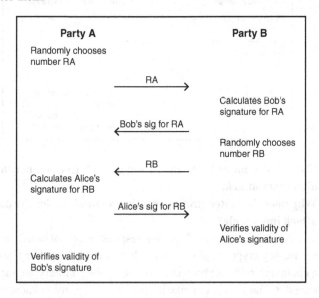

Find a way for Eve to convince Bob and Alice that they are talking to each other when in fact they are each talking to Eve.

5. We describe a protocol proposed in 1989 for enabling people to communicate privately in a radio network. The protocol uses a trusted center to

handle the go-between. In this protocol, we ignore issues of authentication and identification: proving who you are is not necessary.

This protocol requires that only the trusted center have an RSA public-key/private-key pair. All other parties know the public key of the trusted center, and none of them knows the corresponding secret key.

Here is how the protocol goes. Suppose party A wants to communicate privately with party B.

(a) Party A chooses a big random key R, encrypts R using the trusted center's public key, and sends the cyphertext to the trusted center.

(b) The trusted center informs party B of the request.

(c) Party B chooses a big random session key K, encrypts K using the trusted center's public key, and sends the cyphertext to the trusted center.

(d) The trusted center decrypts the cyphertext from A, obtaining the key R, and decrypts the cyphertext from B, obtaining the key K. It uses the one-time pad to encrypt K using key R (i.e., adds K and R using modular arithmetic), and sends the cyphertext to Party A.

(e) Party A decrypts the cyphertext, obtaining K. Now Party A and Party B have a common key, K, and so they encrypt all their messages to one another using an ordinary (single-key) cryptosystem.

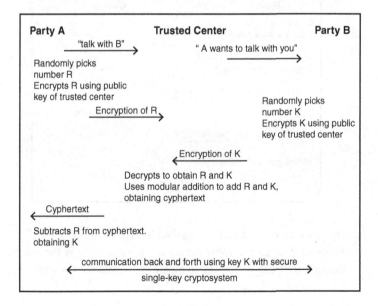

Assume the trusted center behaves honestly. This protocol *seems* quite secure, but has a rather striking weakness. Two parties C and D working together and eavesdropping on all communication can arrange to decrypt the communication between A and B.

Your job is to figure out how.

Hint 1: After eavesdropping on the communication between A, B, and the trusted center, C requests to communicate with D.

6. Consider an Internet roulette game. A player places a bet, selects one of the numbers 1 through 36, and sends the chosen number to the Internet Casino. The Casino selects one of the numbers (presumably at random!) and then tells the player whether he has won or not. Obviously there is a security problem if the player has to send his chosen number in plaintext form: the Casino can simply avoid that number!

   Here is an apparently better way to implement the roulette game. There is a system-wide one-way function f. Instead of sending his guess, the player uses his guess as the input to f, and calculates the corresponding output and sends it to the Casino. Once the Casino sends the winning number to the player, he tells them his guess. The Casino can then verify for itself that the player is not lying, because it can itself find the image of the alleged guess under f, and verify that it matches what the player sent earlier.

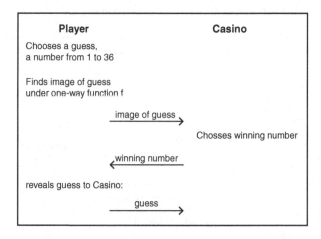

   (a) Describe the biggest security flaw with this system.
   (b) Suppose f is an invertible function whose domain is the numbers 1 through 10^{20}. Suggest a way to repair the system so it is secure.

Further Reading

[1] E. T. Bell. *Men of Mathematics*. New York, NY: Simon and Schuster (1937).

[2] David Kahn. *The Codebreakers: The Story of Secret Writing*, 2nd ed. New York, NY: Scribner (1996).

[3] Peter Wright with Paul Greengrass. *Spycatcher: The Candid Autobiography of a Senior Intelligence Officer*. New York, NY: Viking (1987).

[4] Charlie Kaufman, Radia Perlman, and Mike Speciner. *Network Security: Private Communication in a Public World*. Englewood Cliffs, NJ: Prentice-Hall (1995).

[5] Bruce Schneier. *Applied Cryptography*, 2nd ed. New York, NY: John Wiley & Sons (1996).

[6] Douglas R. Stinson. *Cryptography: Theory and Practice*. Boca Raton, FL: CRC Press (1995).

Index

Printed in the United States
by Baker & Taylor Publisher Services